The Journal
of
Paul

*Devotional Insights into the
Message of the Apostle Paul*

Greece '05

Ed & Bernie,
Thanks for the journey in
Paul's footsteps. God's grace & peace

David L. Sparks

The Journal of Paul

*Devotional Insights into the
Message of the Apostle Paul*

David L. Sparks

ISBN 1-55630-514-1

PUBLISHED BY:
BRENTWOOD CHRISTIAN PRESS
4000 BEALLWOOD AVENUE
COLUMBUS, GEORGIA 31904

Dedication

This book is dedicated to my dear wife, Elizabeth,
for sharing with me her native homeland
and the land of Paul's missionary journeys, Greece,
and to our children, David and Adam
who have crossed the seas with us.

Introduction

Imagine how fascinating it would be if the Apostle Paul had kept a journal recording the events of his life and missionary journeys! What a fascinating journal it would be! F. F. Bruce states:

No single event, apart from the Christ-event itself, has proved so determinant for the course of Christian history as the conversion and commissioning of Paul.
Paul: Apostle of the Heart Set Free

It was Paul who received his commission from the Risen Lord on the Damascus road to be God's servant

"I am Jesus!
I am appointing you as my servant, as my witness..."
Acts 26:16

Paul's focus in life was to proclaim Jesus to those who had never heard of the Savior's grace and love. Indeed, that is what Paul did throughout his days. He was faithful and zealous in his calling. During three missionary journeys, he advanced the Gospel in Asia Minor, Macedonia, and Greece. And in his defense of the Gospel, he even went to the imperial city of Rome to share the message of Jesus Christ before Caesar! His plans also included a trip to Spain. Truly, he was a remarkable man of God!

It was surely from his every day experiences that he developed his understanding of his faith in Christ. It was in the milieu of mainstream society that Paul cultivated his presentation of the Gospel. We see in his letters how he drew upon the various local scenes. He compared the Christian life to the life of an athlete and the training of a soldier. He drew upon the agricultural aspects of his surroundings when speaking of the fruit of the Spirit. In Athens, he used the backdrop of the pagan temples of the Acropolis to present a sermon to "The Unknown God," that God being none other than Jesus Christ. In the best sense of the word, Paul was a man of his times.

Of course, Paul did not leave behind a journal. But drawing upon his letters and the accounts of Luke's *Acts,* I've attempted to fashion one. From my travels in Israel, Turkey (Asia Minor) and Greece, I've walked in Paul's steps and tried to see the world through his eyes. I've tried to recreate the settings in which Paul reflected upon his faith. Throughout this book, Paul's writings have been placed in a real-life setting. Hopefully this will add to the depth and appreciation of his words. But the higher aim is that the reader will be drawn closer to Jesus Christ and so join with Paul in saying:

> *"I have been crucified with Christ*
> *and I no longer live,*
> *but Christ lives in me.*
> *The life I live...*
> *I live by faith in the Son of God,*
> *who loved me*
> *and gave himself for me."*
> **Galatians 2:20**

David Sparks
1998

Contents

Maps

Historical Highlights

Historical Highlight
Chronology of Paul's Life

- Childhood Days in Tarsus, a Roman province of Cilicia
- Youth/Early Manhood in Jerusalem for His education
  Student of the Rabbi Gamaliel
  Member of the Pharisees
- The Witnessing of Stephen's Martyrdom: 32/33
- The Encounter of Jesus on the Damascus Road: 33/34
- A Ministry in Arabia and Damascus: (3 years)
- A Brief Visit to Jerusalem with Barnabas
- Ministry in Cilicia and Syria: The Silent Years (11 years)
- Barnabas and Paul Minister in Antioch
- First Missionary Journey: 47/48
  Cyprus, Perga, Pisidian Antioch, Iconium, Lystra, Derbe,
  Lystra, Iconium, Pisidian Antioch, Pamphylia, Attalia, Antioch
- The Jerusalem Council: 49
  Acceptance of Gentiles
- Second Missionary Journey: 49-52
  Antioch, Syria and Cilicia, Derbe, Lystra, Iconium, Phrygia
  and Galatia, Troas, Philippi, Thessalonica, Berea, Athens,
  Corinth, Ephesus, Caesarea, Antioch
- Third Missionary Journey: 52-56
  Antioch, Galatia & Phrygia, Ephesus, Macedonia and Greece,
  Troas, Miletus, Jerusalem
- The Arrest: 56
  Jerusalem, Caesarea
- Paul's Voyage to Rome: 59/60
  Sidon, Myra, Cnidus, Fair Havens, Malta, Syracuse,
  Rhegium, Puteoli, Forum of Appius, Three Taverns, Rome
- Imprisonment in Roman: 60-62
- Released? Exiled? Extended Travel?
- Imprisonment and Death 64/65

The Journal Entries

Entry 1

Just as in the days of Jesus' ministry there were those who sought to put Him to death, so also were there those who sought to destroy His followers. After Jesus' resurrection and ascension into heaven, the Church faced hostility by the religious rulers of their day. One of those who persecuted them was a Pharisee named Saul. We are told in *Acts* that he went from house to house, dragging off Jesus' followers and putting them into prison. *Acts* also tells us that Saul witnessed the stoning of Stephen, a man full of God's grace and power...

"Saul was there, giving approval to Stephen's death..."
Acts 8:1

It is by no means an accident that Luke records this event and these characters. As Saul witnessed the death of Stephen, he would have seen an amazing testimony of Christ's forgiveness. Did the face of Stephen—a face like the face of an angel—trouble the heart of Saul? Did the words of Stephen, "Lord, do not hold this sin against them" (Acts 7:60) pierce into the soul of Saul? Did the witness of Stephen lead Saul to the Savior? Surely, Saul could not forget the look in Stephen's eyes as he gazed into heaven and saw the glory of God!

Most people will receive their first glimpse of God by looking into the faces of Jesus' followers.
Hopefully, they will see a look of compassion and love.

The Look Lingers On

Acts 7:59; 8:1
Based on Paul's witnessing of the stoning of Stephen.

The look lingers on. . .
I am haunted by his face!
With stones hurling toward him
driving him to the ground
ripping his flesh
bruising his body
battering the breath of life from him. . .
his spirit remains at peace,
his face radiates joy,
his lips whisper a prayer!

"Lord Jesus, receive my spirit. . .
Lord, do not hold this sin against them."
Acts 7:59-60

What words are these?
words of assurance?
words of acceptance?
words of compassion?
words of forgiveness?
Words prayed for those
who heave their hatred upon him
with devastating blows?
How can this be!
It troubles my spirit.
Is there truth in his words?

NO! NO!
NO! NO!

He speaks against the law.
He speaks against the temple.
He deserves the sentence of death.
I shall erase the picture of his face from my mind!

It will haunt me no more!

And yet,
the look lingers on. . .

Prayer

O God,
what is happening to me?

Historical Highlight
The Names: Saul and Paul

"Then Saul, who was also called Paul..."
Acts 13:9

As a citizen within the Roman Empire, the Apostle Paul had three names—
• a forename,
• a family name,
• and an additional name that was used in daily life.

Of these three types of names, only his common name of daily life is known. In the Greek, his name was Paul (Paulos). This was the name he used in identifying himself in his letters written to the various churches of the New Testament (Romans 1:1).

We learn of Paul's Jewish name only through the writings of Luke in the book of Acts. When Luke speaks of Paul in the context of the Jerusalem scene, he refers to Paul as Saul. Since the apostle was from the tribe of Benjamin, (the most famous Benjaminite being the first king of Israel, King Saul), and perhaps because of the rhyming qualities of the two names, Saul and Paul appear to be interchangeable depending upon the setting, i.e., Jewish or Gentile. Luke's first usage of the name Paul appears in Acts 13:13 as Paul and Barnabas left the island of Cyprus and began their first missionary journey among the Greco-Roman world in the region of Asia Minor (modern Turkey.) From this point on, Luke consistently refers to Paul using his Greek name.

14

Entry 2

Saul's heart was in turmoil. He had witnessed the death of Stephen and had seen the grace in his eyes. Yet his mind told him that Stephen was a blasphemer who spoke against the Law and the Temple and deserving of death. Saul could not reconcile his heart and his head. He was at war within himself. And the greater the battle within, the greater the havoc he brought upon the Church. Wherever Saul went, he breathed out murderous threats against Jesus' followers.

One day, while he was on a mission to Damascus to arrest the followers of the "Way," Saul encountered a blinding light that drove him to his knees. It was on his knees that Saul first met Jesus!

At times, being in the right position allows us to meet Jesus. Often, that position is on our knees!

I am Jesus

Acts 9; 22; 26
Based on the conversion of Saul on the Damascus road.

A penetrating light
slashed through the heavens. . .
shining brighter than the sun
blazing like a furnace
striking my eyes
driving me to the ground!

On my knees,
I stared into the light
and a voice called out my name. . .

> **"Saul! Saul!**
> **Why do you persecute me!"**

Who is this one whose voice I hear?
Speak to me!
Who are you?

> **"I am Jesus"**

Jesus?
How can this be?
You were crucified,
nailed to a cross
placed in a grave.
Tell me, I demand it, who are you?

> *Once again came the reply. . .*
> **"I am Jesus of Nazareth"**

Jesus of Nazareth?
Can this be so?
Can it be that the testimonies of those I persecute is true?
That the one who died, now lives?
Who are you, Lord?

> **"Jesus of Nazareth,**
> **Why do you persecute me?"**

Jesus, the Righteous One spoken of by Stephen?

Acts 8:52

The one whose face he saw is now
the one whose face I see.
    I hear your voice
        I see your face
           It is true.
What shall I do?
And he spoke words with a strange message. . .

> **"I am appointing you as**
> **a servant**
> **and a witness.**
> **I'm sending you to the world**
> **to open blind eyes;**
> **to turn the people**
> **from darkness to light;**
> **to turn them from the**
> **power of evil to the power of God.**
> **Tell them of my forgiveness!**
> **Bring them to me!"**
> Acts 26:16-18

> **"My ears had heard of you**
> **but now my eyes have seen you."**
> Job 42:5

17

Prayer

Gracious God,
Today, salvation has come
*   into this life of mine.*
Today, for the first day in my life,
*   I know that the testimony is true.*
*   Jesus is the Risen Lord.*
My struggle is over;
My doubts are gone.

You know me by name, and now,
*   I am forever yours.*

Amazing grace that saved
*   a wretch like me!*

Amen.

Achaia: During the time of Paul, this name was used to refer to the southern province of Greece that included the cities of Corinth, Athens, and Cenchreae. II Corinthians 1:1; I Thessalonians 1:8.

Antioch in Syria: Second only to Jerusalem, Antioch served as a major center of the early church. Barnabas and Paul ministered in this community for a whole year. In this city, the disciples were first called "Christians" (Acts 11:26). Paul began and ended his first and second missionary journeys from the seaport of Antioch. His third journey also began from this city.

Athens: Athens was visited by Paul during his second journey. Paul delivered his famous sermon, "To The Unknown God," while standing before the council of Athens known as the Areopagus. Acts 17:16-32.

Berea: After a riot in Thessalonica instigated by the synagogue, Paul and Silas, under cover of night, made their way to Berea. While in Berea, Paul once again preached in the synagogue, explaining from the scriptures daily that Jesus had to suffer and die and rise from the dead and that He was the Messiah. One of Paul's traveling companions, Sopater, was from Berea. Acts 17:11; Acts 20:4.

Corinth: Corinth, located on the Peloponnese Peninsula, boasted two harbors, Lachaeum on the Gulf of Corinth, and Cenchreae on the Saronic Gulf. It was a leading center of commerce and industry, particularly ceramics. Paul's ministry in Corinth lasted a significant amount of time, 18-months, during which he labored as a tentmaker with coworkers Aquila and Priscilla. Acts 18:1-18

Damascus: This leading city of Syria was the destination of Saul as he set out to persecute the followers of Christ. Following his conversion, Paul preached his first sermon as an apostle of Christ in Damascus. Acts 9:2, 10, 19.

Ephesus: Ephesus was the most important city in the Roman province of Asia. It also served as the headquarters of Paul for a period of approximately three years. Acts 18:18-21; 19.

Galatia: Galatia was a Roman province located in Asia Minor. Within the province were towns Paul evangelized on his first missionary travels: Antioch, Iconium, Lystra, and Derbe. Acts 13-14.

Macedonia: Macedonia was a kingdom in what is today northern Greece. The most renowned Macedonian king was Alexander the Great (4th c. BC). Paul, in response to a vision from the Lord, sailed to Macedonia from the port of Troas. He founded churches in Philippi, Thessalonica, and Berea. Acts 16:9; I Thessalonians 1:7.

Philippi: This city of Macedonia derived its name from the father of Alexander the Great, Philip II, who reestablished this city in 360 BC. In 42 BC the famous battle with Antony and Octavian against Brutus and Cassius was waged on the plains of Philippi. Paul and Silas were imprisoned here during their second missionary journey. The church at Philippi was a strong supporter of Paul and his ministry. Acts 16; Philippians 1:7.

Rome: This city was founded in 753 BC on its seven hills. It was the center of the Roman Empire and the seat of the senate and of the Caesarian administration. During the New Testament period, Rome was a cosmopolitan city with a population over a million. Paul's letter to the Romans differs from his other letters in that it is less personal but more systematic and theological. After Paul was arrested in Jerusalem and put on trial, he appealed his case to Caesar. As a result, Paul's case was transferred to Rome. His journey to Rome was by ship. Acts concludes its life of Paul with Paul under house arrest but free to preach about the Lord Jesus Christ. Acts 25:11; Acts 28:30-31.

Tarsus: This city was located on the Cilician plain and just inland from the Asia Minor coast. It was the home of Paul during his childhood. Tarsus was a meeting place between East and West and served Paul well as he carried the gospel from its eastern roots within Judaism into the western world of the Gentiles. Acts 9:30; Acts 11:25

Thessalonica: Thessalonica was the leading city of Macedonia during the time of Paul. Its geography served it well as it sat on the major land route from Italy to the east as well as the main route from the Aegean to the Danube. Soon after his departure from the city during his second journey, Paul penned two letters to this congregation encouraging them to serve as a model Christian community. I Thessalonians 1:8.

Troas: Located on the coast of north-western Asia Minor, Troas (approximately 12 miles from ancient Troy), it was the crossing port from Asia Minor to Macedonia. Paul received his Macedonia vision while in Troas. Later, on his third journey and in Troas once again, Paul raised Eutychus from the dead after the youth fell from an upper story window. Acts 16:9-10; 20:7-12.

Entry 3

Jesus once said,

> *"I have come into this world,*
> *so that the blind will see*
> *and those who see will become blind."*
> John 9:39

He was saying that those who are aware of their need are those who can have their eyes opened; those who do not realize they cannot see are those who are truly blind and beyond hope and help.

It was when Saul became blind, that, for the first time in his life, he could truly see! The darkness that covered his eyes for three days led to the dawning of a new day. With his blindness, Saul had to let others lead him by the hand.

❖

The first step in learning to see is taken
when we learn to trust!

Blind Eyes

Acts 9:8-9
Based on the three days Paul waited in darkness.

Blind eyes. . .
A darkness falls upon me as I've never known before.

> *As a little child,*
> *I grasp for*
>> *a hand to hold me,*
>> *a hand to lead me,*
>> *a hand to keep me safe,*
>> *a hand to comfort me!*
>>> Acts 9:7-9

> *Gone are*
>> *my sure steps*
>> *my self-determination*
>> *my assertiveness*
>> *my independence*
>> *my haughtiness*
>> *my pride.*

As a little child learning to walk,
I, too, am learning to walk,
> *but. . .*
> *not by sight but by faith.*
>> II Corinthians 5:7

Prayer

Lord,

Take my hand,
    Take my days;
Lead my steps,
    Light my way.

The One who calls,
    He knows my name.
The crucified Lord
    Suffered my pain.

In this darkness
    As my sight grows dim;
Give me new eyes
    To see only Him.

       Amen.

Entry 4

During his three days of waiting in the house on Straight Street in Damascus, Saul must have felt very alone. No longer would he be accepted by his fellow Pharisees. *Acts* tells us that, when they learned of the news of Saul's conversion, they conspired to kill him.

And those Saul was called by the Risen Christ to serve were afraid of him. They knew him as the one who had tried to arrest, imprison, and destroy them.

Waiting alone, Saul must have felt all alone.

And then a man, sent by God, came to him, placed his arm around him, and called to him—"brother Saul." At that moment, the darkness of loneliness was lifted.

God still calls us to reach out to those
who feel alone and receive them
as our brothers and as our sisters.

Brother Saul

Acts 9:10-18
Based on the meeting between Saul and Ananias.

In my blindness,
I received a vision. . .
> *A man approaches.*
> *He puts his hands upon me,*
> *and then he speaks.*
So I waited in this house on the street called Straight;
> *three days, neither eating nor drinking...*

On the third day,
> *I heard a knock at the door.*
>> *footsteps crossed the room,*
>> *someone's hand rested upon my head,*
>> *and then I heard his voice. . .*
And his words filled my ears with amazement!
> *His first words!*
>> ***"Brother Saul!"***

He called me, "brother!"
Just three days ago,
I was in pursuit of these people of "The Way."

My purpose was
> *to hunt them down*
> *and root them out,*
> *to arrest and persecute them,*
> *and condemn and destroy them.*

The reputation of my hostility was known to all!
In the ears of those who heard it,
> *my name struck fear into their hearts.*
My voice was full of murderous threats,
My spirit was filled with rage...

And yet, this man named Ananias
did not fear me,
did not condemn me,
did not revile me,
did not judge me. . .

Instead, he called me his brother,
showering me with brotherly love. . .
"Brother Saul!"

Such amazing acceptance,
Such unspoken forgiveness.
He spoke to me as if I were his long lost brother...
no bitterness was in his voice;
it was full of compassion and love.
His spirit spoke of forgiveness,
my hatred was forgiven,
my rage was forgiven,
I was forgiven...
He called me, "brother!"

The psalmist wrote of it;
Today I experienced it...

"How good and pleasant it is when brothers
live together in unity!
It is like precious oil poured on the head,
running down on the beard,
running down on Aaron's beard,
down upon the collar of his robes.
It is as if the dew of Hermon were falling
on Mount Zion.
For there the Lord bestows his blessings,
even life forevermore."
Psalm 133

Prayer

I praise You Lord, with all my soul;
All my inmost being praises Your holy name.

I praise You Lord with all my soul;
And I shall never forget all Your benefits.

You forgive all my sins
*   and heal all my diseases;*
You redeem my life from the pit
*   and crown me with love and compassion.*
You do not deal with me as my sins deserve,
*   or repay me according to my iniquities.*

For as high as the
heavens are above the earth,
So great is Your love for me;
As far as the
east   is from the   west,
so far have You removed
my transgressions from me.
I praise You Lord,
with all my soul!
Psalm 103

Amen.

Entry 5

Throughout the ages, I Corinthians, chapter thirteen, has been on the list of favorite Scriptural passages. It is Paul's beautiful description of God's love, and is often referred to as "The Love Chapter."

If Paul were called upon to describe the face of Christ that he witnessed on the road to Damascus, he could not choose any better words than those found in this chapter. Many have discovered that by replacing the word 'love' with the name of Jesus, they have found a perfect portrait of the Savior.

The most excellent way to demonstrate the presence of God in our lives, wrote the Apostle Paul, is to pursue the way of love—God's love made manifest in Jesus Christ.

If others are to see Jesus in us,
our love must always protect,
always trust, always hope,
always persevere, always endure.

The Face of Christ
I Corinthians 13
Based on Paul's portrait of Jesus.

So often,
I've tried to describe
> *the face of my Savior*
> *the face of the one who looked*
> *at me with compassion*
> *on the day of my calling.*

It is impossible to speak of the love in his eyes.
Words are inadequate to speak
of the kindness in his look...
> *I struggle for the right words.*
> *There is only one word. . .*
>> *Love!*

A love that is patient and kind;
A love that is humble and meek.
A love that is gracious and merciful;
A love that is full of forgiveness.
A love that always protects,
> *always trusts,*
> *always hopes,*
> *always perseveres.*
A love that never fails.
> I Corinthians 13:4-8

How wide
> *and long*
>> *and high*
>> *and deep*
>>> *is the love of Christ!*
>> Ephesians 3:18

This is the portrait of Jesus.
This is the look that radiated
 from his face.

The look of love.
I shall never forget his face...

Prayer

Great is your love,
O God, my Savior.
Your love endures forever.

No eye has seen,
No ear has heard,
No mind has conceived
 how great is Your love for us. . .
  even for me.
   I Corinthians 2:9

Amen.

Historical Highlight
Approximate Order of Paul's Letters*

Galatians	49
I Thessalonians	50-51
II Thessalonians	50-51
I Corinthians	54
II Corinthians	55
Romans	55
Ephesians	60
Colossians	60
Philemon	60
Philippians	61
I Timothy	62
Titus	62
II Timothy	63

*The dates of writing are still under discussion by various scholars.

Entry 6

In his years of ministry, Paul could boast of many great accomplishments. He led countless people to trust in Jesus Christ and founded numerous churches throughout Asia Minor and Greece. He penned letters filled with keen theological insights that still demand attention today. He boldly proclaimed the Gospel before such audiences as the Council of Athens, the court of the Roman governor of Judea, Felix, and possibly before the Emperor of Rome.

Through the centuries Paul has been praised as a great theologian, evangelist, missionary, church planter, ambassador, etc. But if you asked Paul how he would best like to be remembered, his answer would surely be, "I, Paul, have become a servant of Jesus Christ."

Jesus said,

> *"For the Son of Man did not come to be served,*
> *but to serve,*
> *and to give his life as a ransom for many."*
> Matthew 20:28

For those in the Kingdom of God,
there is no greater status and no greater privilege
than to be a servant of Jesus Christ.

A Servant

Colossians 1:23
Based upon Paul's address to the church at Colosse.

I struggle with a word to describe
my call in Christ--

~~ambassador~~	II Corinthians 5: 20
~~proclaimer~~	Colossians 4: 3
~~leader~~	Acts 13: 2
~~laborer~~	Philippians 2: 16
~~apostle~~	Romans 1: 1
~~church planter~~	Acts 14: 21-22
~~speaker~~	Acts 13: 16
~~writer~~	I Corinthians 16: 21
~~representative~~	II Thessalonians 3: 7
~~missionary~~	Romans 1: 5-6
~~teacher~~	Ephesians 4: 21-22
~~messenger~~	II Thessalonians 3: 1
~~testifier~~	II Timothy 1: 8
~~planner~~	Acts 15: 36
~~preacher~~	I Corinthians 1: 23
~~reconciler~~	II Corinthians 5: 8
~~comforter~~	II Corinthians 1: 4
~~minister~~	II Corinthians 3: 6
~~worker~~	II Corinthians 6: 1

I've found the word!

SERVANT!
Colossians 1:23

Paul, a servant of Jesus Christ!

36

Once I was alienated from God
   and an enemy of Christ;
Now I have been reconciled to God
   through the death of Christ.

This is the Gospel that I shall proclaim
   to every creature under heaven; this is the Gospel of
   which I, Paul, have become a servant!

            I am a servant of Christ Jesus,
               called to be an apostle
            and set apart for the gospel of God...

Prayer

      Gracious and merciful Father, make me a servant.

                  Give me the
                  attitude of
                  Jesus Christ,
                  who, being in
      very nature God, did not consider equality with You
      something to be grasped, but made himself nothing,
            taking the very nature of a servant,
                  being made
                  in human
                  likeness,
                  being found
                  in appearance
                  as a man,
                  he humbled
                  himself
                  and became
                  obedient
                  to death..
                  even death
                  on a cross.
                Philippians 2:6-8
                  Amen

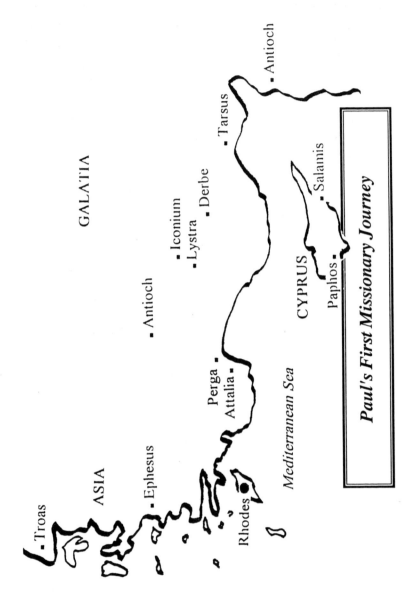

Paul's First Missionary Journey

GALATIA

Troas

ASIA

Ephesus

Antioch

Iconium

Lystra

Derbe

Tarsus

Antioch

Perga

Attalia

Rhodes

Mediterranean Sea

CYPRUS

Salamis

Paphos

Entry 7

As a Pharisee, Paul had conducted his life by the dictates of the Law of Moses. According to his testimony, he considered his former life as one that was blameless before the Law. But that was before he understood the holiness of God—that God's standard of holiness was not based upon the outward observance of codified regulations but upon the condition of a person's heart. Although he still valued the Law, Paul no longer saw himself as its slave. Christ had set him free through the power of a new birth.

But there were some within the Jerusalem church who insisted that all Gentiles entering the fellowship of the saints must be circumcised and held accountable to the Law of Moses. Their plan of salvation demanded obedience to the customs and ceremonies of Israel. Around the necks of new believers, they sought to place the yoke of the Law—a yoke that not even they nor their fathers had been able to bear. From his days as a strict observer of the Law and as a Pharisee, Paul knew the folly of such fanaticism. Salvation was not based upon human endeavors, but upon the work of Jesus Christ; not upon obedience to regulations but upon the righteousness of Christ.

"Nothing in my hand I bring,
Only to the cross I cling."

Unthinkable

Acts 15 and Romans 3 and Galatians 2
Based on Paul's visit to the church at Jerusalem.

"Unthinkable!" they say.
"The Law of Moses must be obeyed!"
"This, too, is a requirement for salvation!"
Acts 15:1

The Law!
I have spent my whole life keeping the Law!
  as for legalistic righteousness. . .faultless!
  as a keeper of the traditions. . .extremely zealous!

Outwardly, my life was blameless,
  but
Inwardly, my life was in turmoil.

Sin reigned within my spirit!
Others may see the outward appearance,
    but it is the Lord who looks at the heart!
I Samuel 16:7

All my outward acts were as filthy rags for they came
    from a heart turned against God!
All my attempts to reach perfection were futile strivings
    to impress a righteous and holy God.

My acts,
my attempts,
    they all fell short of the glory of God.
Romans 3:23

The Law did not save me
   but only served to show me that
      there is none
      who is righteous before God.

It was JESUS who set me free!
   While I was still a sinner,
   Christ died for me!

He justified me freely by his blood!
He redeemed me from the curse of the Law!

                    It is through
                    the grace
                    of our Lord Jesus
                    that we are saved!
                    Acts 15:11

Saved under the Law?
Unthinkable!

Prayer

Gracious God,
   When the time had fully come,
      you sent your son,
         born of a woman,
            born under the law,
               to redeem me
                  as one under the law,
                     that I might receive
                        your grace.   Galatians 4:4

May I, in gratitude, live all my days for you!
May I be crucified with Christ that I might no longer live,
but Christ might live in me! Galatians 2:20

This I pray in the name of the Son of God,
who loved me and gave himself for me!
                    Amen.

41

Entry 8

Within the Christian community there are times and events that don't speak well of our life in Christ. Even among the leadership, there are situations that speak more about human sinfulness than about God's righteousness. Such was the case between Paul and Barnabas.

These men were the best of friends. For Paul, Barnabas was a source of great encouragement. For Barnabas, Paul was a man with keen insights into the mind and heart of God. Together in ministry, they made a dynamic team. For years they served together side by side.

But one day, a disagreement came between them. As the two men made plans for a missionary journey, Barnabas suggested they take with them a young man named Mark. Mark had traveled with the two on an earlier journey, but had left during the expedition. It was for this reason Paul had no desire for Mark to join them on their second journey. And so a rift developed among these two pillars of God. Paul went his way; Barnabas and Mark went their way. The outcome was that two dynamic ministries grew out of the one.

God has a way of transforming even our human failures
into a blessing for the kingdom.

Parting Company
Acts 15:36-41
Based on the split between Paul and Barnabas.

From the day we met,
it was easy to understand why your
name was changed from
Joseph to Barnabas
      (which means Son of encouragement)
                  Acts 4:36

You have been, for me,
      a strong source of encouragement!
You are a good man,
      full of the Holy Spirit, abounding in faith,
      steadfast and true, my closest of friends—
Barnabas!
                  Acts 11:24

Upon my conversion,
      when everyone looked at me
      with fearful eyes and suspicious minds
            (with every right to do so!),
you were there for me,
      standing with me,
      and testifying to God's gracious transformation in my life.
                  Acts 9:27

The Spirit has blessed our joint ministries.
In Antioch, when we taught together. . .
      (I remember that while there,
      Barnabas coined the term "Christians"
      to describe us as the disciples of Christ)
                  Acts 11:25-26

God's grace was evident to all.
You have always shared your faith with conviction, with
great compassion, and with immense patience.
I find nothing but good words with which to praise you as
a servant of our Savior and Lord Jesus Christ.

Yet, today we have parted company.
You wanted to take Mark, your nephew, with us in our
journeys. I was not in favor of this decision.

Unfortunately,
we disagreed rather disagreeably. . .
And this is what pains me!

We have spent too many years together to let this rift
come between us. . .
I am afraid it has done so!

At times. . .
I don't understand what I do.
For what I want to do I do not do,
      but what I hate I do.
I have the desire to do what is good,
      but I cannot carry it out.
It is sin living in me!

Romans 7:15-20

Relationships!
They are the true marks of the life in Christ,
And yet they are so difficult!

It's not easy learning to forgive and be forgiven.
It's so difficult exercising patience with others
      and yet I want others to be patient with me!

Prayer

Compassionate and Forgiving God,
Your words are like honey in the honey-comb
and yet my words are bitter and biting.
You are so patient with me,
and yet so easily I snap at others.
You look to build up and bring out the best in me
and yet I seek to tear down and destroy others.
Your heart is full of mercy
and yet, at times, my heart is like a stone.

In my inner being
I delight in your ways,
and yet, so often, in my relationships
my life is a prisoner of sin.

What a wretched man I am!
Who will rescue me from this body of death?

Thanks be to God. . .
through Jesus Christ my Lord!
Romans 7:24

Gracious Lord,
full of compassion and forgiveness,
before the sunsets,
give me your grace so that I may go
and reconcile myself with Barnabas.
Ephesians 4:26

Even if we part company,
let us do so as brothers in Christ!
For your sake
and the sake of our Savior,

Amen.
46

Historical Highlight
Paul's Inner Circle

Barnabas: "Barnabas" was the name given him by the Apostles. His actual name was Joseph, a Levite from Cyprus. In 48 Barnabas and Paul began their first missionary journey through Asia Minor. Acts 4:36; 9:27; 13:1.

John Mark: His mother's house was a meeting place of the early Christian community in Jerusalem. Peter went to this home after his miraculous release from prison. He was the cousin of Barnabas and joined in the first missionary journey. Although he was the source of a disagreement between Barnabas and Paul, the rift was resolved as Paul later called Mark, "fellow-worker." Later in life he joined Peter in Rome. Acts 12:12, 25; 13:13; 15:37.

Luke: Early tradition testifies that Luke was a Greek physician before being converted. He joined Paul at Troas during the second missionary journey. He also traveled with Paul to Rome during which time he was shipwrecked with Paul on Malta and imprisoned with him in Rome. After Paul's death, he wrote his two-volume work on the life of Jesus, *The Gospel of Luke*, and the growth of the early church, *The Acts of the Apostles*. Colossians 4:14; II Timothy 4:11.

Priscilla & Aquila: They had been expelled from Rome by the emperor Claudius in 49. They settled in Corinth. As fellow tentmakers, they opened their home to Paul when he arrived in this community. During his extended stay in Ephesus, Paul was once again joined by this remarkable couple who "risked their lives" for him. Acts 18:18; Romans 16:3; I Corinthians 16:19; II Timothy 4:19.

Silas: First mentioned at the Council of Jerusalem. Journeyed with Paul for three years on the second missionary campaign. Ministered in Corinth after Paul left for Ephesus. Later in life, he joined Peter in Rome. Acts 15:40; 16:19, 25, 29.

Timothy: A young man from Lystra in Asia Minor. His father was Greek, his mother was a Jew. He joined Paul and Silas during their second journey, often serving as Paul's envoy. Acts 16:1; 17:14; Romans 16:21; II Timothy 1:2.

Titus: Titus served with Paul for longer than any other fellow-worker, a period of 20 years. Titus was born a Gentile. When many in Jerusalem insisted he be circumcised, Paul defended Titus "not giving in to them for a moment, so that the truth of the gospel might remain with you." Titus served with Paul in mediating Paul's relationship with the Christians at Corinth who were practicing immorality. Titus later became the first bishop of Crete. Paul addressed a personal letter to him, describing the qualities of a good bishop. II Corinthians 7:6, 13-14; Titus 1:4.

Entry 9

God works in mysterious ways. What some see as catastrophic, God sees as a means to further a person's growth in faith and trust. What some see as set-backs, God sees as opportunities for the manifestation of grace.

When Paul was arrested and thrown into prison, some saw it as a hindrance to his missionary endeavors. But Paul saw his situation through the eyes of God. When writing to the Philippians, he noted that his arrest by the authorities really served to advance the gospel. Because of his imprisonment the entire palace guard (numbering in the thousands) benefited. Among them he was able to proclaim the Good News of Jesus Christ.

And that was not the only benefit resulting from his arrest. As others in the Christian community witnessed Paul's courageous testimony to the grace and mercy of God even in trying and difficult circumstances, they, too, began fearlessly to tell the message of God's salvation. What many saw as a deterrent to the advance of the gospel was actually a double-blessing. Such being the case, Paul rejoiced to see the mysterious hand of God at work in his life and the lives of others, notwithstanding the circumstances.

God works all things together for our good.
The mystery is that we doubted such was so in the first place!

Words of Comfort
Acts 16:16-34
Based upon Paul's imprisonment in Philippi.

Silas and I have been beaten
*   and yet we are not beaten down!*
We have been thrown into prison
*   and yet our spirits are not imprisoned!*
We have been confined by chains
*   and yet our hearts are free*
*   to soar into the presence of God!*

In the midst of our "den," Silas suggested we speak to one
another with psalms, hymns, and spiritual songs. . .
making music in our hearts to the Lord.
                                        Ephesians 5:19, 20
He has always had a love for music.
He shared with me the words of the Psalmist:

"For when the cords of death entangled me and the
anguish of the grave surrounded me,
the Lord turned his ear to me and heard my cry.
When I was overcome with troubles of every sort,
and sorrow weighed heavily
upon my innermost being,
I called on the name of the Lord—
O Lord, save me!
How wonderful is our Lord,
full of compassion
gracious beyond measure
righteous in all his ways!"
                            Psalm 116

O how the psalmist's words lifted my heart!

Together, Silas and I gave thanks to God the Father for
everything through the precious name
of our Lord Jesus Christ. . .
> *even the stripes we bear upon our backs.*

As we were singing, our chorus was interrupted by a
sudden tremor.
The earth beneath us began to shake.
Our chains rattled loose from their moorings.
Our stocks splintered and cracked.
The prison doors flew open wide.
An earthquake was setting us free!

Little did we know that the tune we were just singing from the
psalms would be repeated by none other than our jailer—
> *but in a cry of desperation!*
> ***"Save me!"***

Our jailer, seeing the prison doors open and fearing that
those under his watch had escaped, had his sword drawn to
take his life.
Knowing that a Roman execution would await him if even one
prisoner escaped, he thought it better to quickly end his life by
his own hand than have it taken from him.

In his last moment of despair came his woeful cry. . .
> ***"Save me!"***

Surely it was God's Spirit that had prompted Silas to
recite the psalmist's cry for deliverance and salvation!
> ***"O Lord, save me!"***

In unison, we called out to the jailer—
> ***"You will be saved!***
> ***By believing in the Lord Jesus!"***

We shared with him the word of the Lord—
and once again God's Spirit was present.
A life was delivered from the dungeon of dread and
brought into the freedom of God's grace.
The jailer was so overwhelmed with his newly found joy
that he insisted that we go with him to his house.
He wanted his entire household to join
the family of the living God.

We drew water from a nearby cistern and baptized both
the jailer and those of his family.
Every one was filled with joy!

Once again we sang the song of the psalmist—
"How wonderful is our Lord.
full of compassion
gracious beyond measure
righteous in all his ways!"

Prayer

O gracious God, O Lord and King
I lift my voice, my gift I bring!
From rising sun, 'til end of day
I give to you eternal praise:

Your hear my voice, my anguished cry
You hear my call, my deepest sigh
And save me with your hand so strong
So I shall sing the eternal song:

How awesome are your deeds;
How mysterious are your ways.
My lips, they shall extol your name
And praise you all my days!
Amen!

Entry 10

There are certain people whose warmth and charm flow from them like a bubbling spring. Such was the dear saint of God, Lydia. *Acts* tells us that as she heard the Good News of Jesus' love, "the Lord opened her heart." These words capture well the spirit of Lydia—a woman with an open heart!

Lydia's first deed after her baptism was to open her home to Paul and his companion, Silas, along with Luke and young Timothy.

After Paul and Silas were released from the prison of Philippi (see Acts 16), they once again went to the house with an open door policy—Lydia's home. Her house had become the meeting place for all the believers. Luke tells us that Lydia's home had a wonderful reputation. It was known as a place of encouragement.

The text does not give many details about Lydia's life, but if it did, it would surely tell us how Lydia's "open heart and open door" ministered to many—perhaps even the poor slave girl from whom Paul exorcised an evil spirit. Did Lydia nurture this abused young women? Did Lydia show her the kindness and goodness of God and help her discover her true worth as one for whom Christ died? It would surprise no one to learn that such was the case from this remarkable woman named Lydia.

Those with an open heart always have an open door.

An Open Heart

Acts 16:11-15
Based on Paul's stay in Philippi on his second journey.

Dearest Lydia,
As it was said of the great people throughout the Scriptures...
"They were of God's own heart,"
so, too, can this be said of you!

There, by the riverside,
seeking to know the way to God,
praying to discern the will of God,
desiring to be drawn closer into the presence of God,
it happened...
the Lord opened your heart!
Acts 16:14

And your heart has remained opened
in ways beyond number.
Your hospitality shall not be forgotten!
such a table, such a feast!
such warm and comfortable surroundings!
such a gentle spirit!

With words of kindness
With deeds of mercy
With acts of Christ's love;
You opened your heart to us!

Your compassion shall not be forgotten!
When no one else cared for the poor slave girl
abused by wicked men
used by the greed of men
and possessed by evil spirits—

When everyone saw her as an outcast,
you took her into your home
you welcomed her as a sister in the Lord
you restored her dignity.
You became a mother to her,
teaching her
self-control and purity
kindness and goodness
and reverence towards God.
Titus 2:5

You served as an example to Jesus' unselfish love. . .
giving beyond measure
giving without demand
giving because of grace!

Your heart is truly an open heart!

Prayer

Gracious God,

Thank you for your servant, Lydia.
From her heart,
may blessings continue to flow!
Through her life,
may Jesus shine.
Thank you for opening her heart to us;

And may my heart be opened to others,
sharing the love of Jesus,
my Savior and Lord.

Amen.

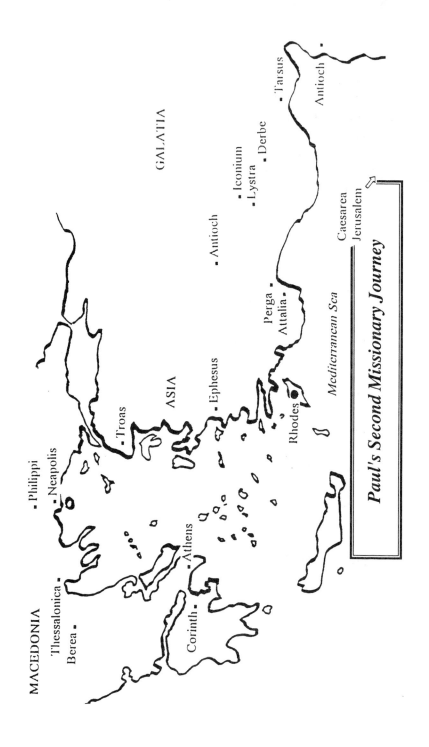

Paul's Second Missionary Journey

MACEDONIA

Philippi
Neapolis
Thessalonica
Berea

Troas

ASIA

Ephesus

Athens

Corinth

Rhodes

GALATIA

Antioch

Iconium
Lystra
Derbe

Tarsus

Antioch

Perga
Attalia

Mediterranean Sea

Caesarea
Jerusalem

Entry 11

Words are never sufficient to stand on their own. They find their true strength when they are acted upon in the matrix of life. For Paul, this was the message he shared with the Christian community of Thessalonica. The demonstration of the transforming power of the Gospel would be seen best as it was lived out in the relationships the Christian community had with others; treating others with patience and kindness; never returning wrong for wrong, but overcoming good with evil; rejoicing in all circumstances; encouraging others in love.

Paul knew that such a life was possible only through the power of the Spirit of God. It was God's Spirit within the believers that would sanctify them through and through—in spirit, soul and body.

The Spirit-filled life finds its strength
as it overflows in active love towards others.

Sanctify Me, Lord
Acts 17:1-9
Based on Paul's stay in Thessalonica.

Thessalonica!
Cosmopolitan city. . .
> *center of politics, culture, commerce*
> *your harbor, the best in the Aegean*
> *your population, the largest in Macedonia.*

*Merchants traverse from east and west on the **Via Egnatia**, the masterful thoroughfare stretching across the vast regions of the Roman Empire.*

All the world is gathered here!
> *laborers, tradesmen,*
> *artisans, craftsmen,*
> *politicians, bureaucrats,*
> *civic officials, philosophers,*
> *teachers, academicians,*
> *the Egyptian religions of*
> *Isis and Serapis,*
> *the Greek cults of*
> *Dionysus and Cabiri,*
> *the Roman deities of every kind.*

As I bring Christ to this city, I bring Christ to the world!
I Thessalonians 1:8

What will convince the inhabitants of this city
> *to turn from sin*
> *to abandon their immoral ways*
> *to seek after God*
> *to come to Christ?*

Will my words change their lives?
        eloquent words?
        persuasive speech?
        rational argument?

Mere words are never enough!
They must see changed lives,
        sanctified lives, holy lives!

The world will be indifferent towards the Gospel
        if my life is not different,
        if God's people are not different!

Prayer

Spirit of holiness,

May I lead my life
    As You would have me do;
May others see the joy
    That comes from knowing You.

When others see my life,
    May I bring You no disgrace.
Make me different, Lord,
    Make Christ seen in my face!

May I be like Christ;
    May I speak His words of grace.
May I show His love;
    May I faithfully run the race!

    Sanctify me, Lord!
    Change me through and through.
    Sanctify me, Lord!
        A living witness for You!

Sanctify my whole spirit, soul, and body;
Fill me with your joy, always,
keep me continually in an attitude of prayer,
may gratitude pour from my life,
in all circumstances;
for this is your will for me in Christ Jesus.

The One who calls me is faithful
and will do it.
I Thessalonians 5:16-24

Amen.

Historical Highlight
Key Themes in Paul's Writings

Grace: God's unearned love at work through Jesus Christ for the salvation of sinful people. The extravagant goodness of God to undeserving people.

> *"But because of his great love for us, God who is rich in mercy, made us alive with Christ even when we were dead in transgressions—it is by grace you have been saved."*
>
> Ephesians 2:4-5

Justification: A term used within the legal system. Pardon from the sentence of sin and death based upon the righteous obedience of Jesus.

> *"Jesus our Lord was delivered over to death for our sins and was raised to life for our justification."*
>
> Romans 4:25

Reconciliation: A term from the realm of relationships. Restoration of fellowship between God and humankind.

> *"For if, when we were enemies of God, we were reconciled to God through the death of God's Son, how much more, having been reconciled, shall we be saved through his life!"*
>
> Romans 5:10

Redemption: A term coming from the slave-market. Deliverance from the slavery of indwelling sin and the bondage of the law.

> *"For he has rescued us from the dominion of darkness and brought us into the kingdom of the son he loves, in whom we have redemption, the forgiveness of sins."*
>
> Colossians 1:13-14.

Righteousness: Being in a right relationship with God based upon faith in God's salvation graciously established and given by Jesus Christ.

"God made Christ who had no sin to be sin for us, so that in him we might become the righteousness of God."
II Corinthians 5:21.

Salvation: Signifies well-being in all its forms. Salvation means deliverance from the penalty of sin and death as well as restoration of wholeness and newness of life. Salvation is rooted in the death and resurrection of Jesus Christ, the Savior.

"I am not ashamed of the gospel, because it is the power of God for the salvation of everyone who believes..."
Romans 1:16.

Sanctification: The path to holiness. The process of becoming more like Christ through the indwelling presence of the Holy Spirit of God.

"May God himself, the God of peace, sanctify you through and through. May your whole spirit, soul and body be kept blameless at the coming of our Lord Jesus Christ."
I Thessalonians 5:23.

Entry 12

We don't often think of Paul as a man who enjoyed the great outdoors, but if we read his letters with an eye looking for his appreciation of nature, we begin to see Paul's love for God's creation. In the world around him, Paul saw the "eternal power" of God in the billowing seas and the lightning bolts. Gazing at the towering mountain range of Mt. Olympus, Paul reflected upon God's "divine qualities"—God's majesty and greatness. The stars that filled the darkness of the night became for Paul a metaphor for the Christian's calling. He also spoke of the splendor of the sun as he described the Christian's heavenly body.

Paul looked forward to the day when all of creation would be liberated from its bondage to decay and brought into the glorious freedom of God.

Those who know the Creator see His hand in all creation!

The Darkness of Night
Acts 17:10-15
Based on Paul's stay in Berea.

I rest tonight on the foothills of Mt. Olympus.
Here the ancient Greeks worshipped their "gods" who resided
on this magnificent range.

What kinds of "gods" were these?
Those who engaged in betrayal
    deception
    corruption
    debauchery. . .
Those who encouraged
    licentiousness
    promiscuity
    perversities!
Romans 1:24-32

Mt. Olympus, your "gods" are no more,
yet their wicked ways continue!

As is the darkness of this night,
    so is the darkness of this age. . .
    exchanging the glory of God
    for images made to look like
    mortal man and birds and animals and reptiles.
Romans 1:23

And yet...
    the darkness is not without light!
Into the darkness has come a light;

> **On those living in the shadow of death,**
> **a light has dawned.**
> Isaiah 9:2

We are to carry the light into the night.
We are to shine like the stars of heaven,
proclaiming the goodness of God,
exalting the name of the Lord. . .
> *the creator of the sun, moon and stars,*
> *lightning, hail, snow and clouds,*
> *stormy winds and raging seas,*
> *all creatures upon the earth.*

Praise the name of the Lord for
His splendor is above the earth and the heavens!
Psalm 148

Light has come into the world;
> *the glory of the Risen Christ!*

Prayer

God of grace,
> *in the midst of this generation,*

> > *May I shine for you;*
> > *doing everything*
> > *without complaining or arguing*
> > *May I be blameless and pure,*
> > *without fault in this world.*
> > *May I be a guide*
> > *to the blind,*
> > *and a light for those*
> > *who are in the dark.*
> > *May I shine for you*
> > *like the stars in the universe.*
Philippians 2:14-15

Amen.

Zeus/Jupiter   Ruler of Mount Olympus and god of weather.

Hera/Juno   Protector of marriage, married women, children and the home.

Poseidon/Neptune   God of the sea and earthquakes.

Ares/Mars   God of war.

Hermes/Mercury   Messenger of the gods, protector of flocks and cattle, thieves and mischief-makers.

Aphrodite/Venus   Goddess of love and beauty.

Hephaestus/Vulcan   God of fire and artisans.

Dionysus/Bacchus   God of the vine and fertility and hospitality.

Apollo/Apollo   God of the sun and patron of truth, archery, music, medicine and prophecy.

Athena/Minerva   God of wisdom.

Demeter/Ceres   Goddess of crops, giver of grain and fruit.

Artemis/Diana   Goddess of the moon and guardian of cities and women of all ages. Twin sister of Apollo.

Entry 13

When we think of the ancient land of Greece, three names immediately come to mind—Socrates, Plato, Aristotle. Their philosophical thought profoundly shaped the development of the Western world. They sought the meaning of life not through magic or superstition but through the use of man's own reasoning powers. Throughout the history of Greece, philosophical speculation became a way of life, with Athens serving as the leading city of intellectual discourse.

When Paul arrived in Athens, he reasoned with the thinkers of his day—the Epicurean and Stoic philosophers. But Paul's message was different. He presented not a new system of thought for consideration. Instead, he presented a person who

> *"commands people everywhere to repent,*
> *for He has set a day when He will judge*
> *the world with justice."*
> Acts 17:30, 31

Paul was never interested in tickling human ears with fanciful ideas. His intention was always to lead women and men, through repentance, into a relationship with God based upon the redemptive work of Christ. In his letter to the church at Corinth, Paul summarized his message with simple words:

> *"I preach Christ and him Crucified."*
> I Corinthians 2:2

Wisdom comes not from weighty words,
but from the One who was wounded for our transgressions.

Foolish Wisdom

Acts 17:16-34
Based on Paul's stay in Athens on his second journey.

Today I listened to the philosophers in the forum
   seeking to persuade people
      with words,
      and wisdom,
      and witty babble;

tickling human ears with intriguing thoughts;
filling men's minds with speculative ideas about
the proper perspective for achieving
   harmony and beauty,
      with self,
      with others
      with the universe,
      and with the "gods,"

taking people captive through
   hollow and deceptive philosophy,
   dependent on human tradition
   and the basic principles of this world.
                   Colossians 2:8

Empty words. . .
   Futile words. . .
      Powerless words. . .

One time, I, too, lived with the illusion
that words offered salvation for the soul...
   I pored over the Scriptures;
   I devoted myself to the study of the Law.
   I convinced myself that compliance to words
      would make me wise
         would make me holy
            would bring me to God.

Yet, such words
  left me empty inside
  and dead towards God!

                    Galatians 3:10-14

If I deliver a message of mere words,
  I offer nothing. . .
    nothing but false hopes,
    vain imaginings,
    impotent promises.

But the Gospel is not a matter of human words
or worldly wisdom;
It is about power!
God's power!

                    I Corinthians 2:5

The power of the Risen Christ
  to forgive sins!
The power of the Holy Spirit
  to sanctify lives!
The power of God
  to make people alive!

What words are powerless to do, God does!

God brings us
  from darkness into light,   Acts 26:18
  from slavery into freedom,   Romans 6:6
  from death into life.   Romans 6:11

All this through the cross of Christ, my Lord.

Prayer

God of grace,

> *Your foolishness is wiser*
> > *than my wisest thought.*
> *Your weakness is stronger*
> > *than my greatest strength.*

> *May the cross of Christ be*
> > *my source of power and*
> > > *my supply of wisdom!*
> > > > I Corinthians 1:25

> *May I ever cling to the cross*
> > *of the One who died for me*
> > *so that I might walk in newness of life.*

Amen.

Historical Highlight
Poets and Philosophers

Paul was familiar with many of the Greek poets and philosophers. In his address to the council of the Areopagus found in Acts 17, Paul quotes several Greek works of literature:

verse 28

"In him we live and move and have our being."

Epimenides (c. 600 B.C.)

"We are his offspring."

Aratus (c. 315-240 B.C.)

Cleanthes (c. 331-240 B.C.)

Other quotes cited by Paul are found in his letter to the community of Corinth and in his personal correspondence to Titus:

I Corinthians 15:33

"Bad company corrupts good character."

Menander (342-291 B.C.)

comic playwright

Titus 1:12

"Cretans are always liars, evil brutes, lazy gluttons."

Epimenides (c. 600 B.C.)

Whether reciting the prophets of Israel or the poets and philosophers of Greece, Paul was well prepared to present the plan of God's salvation to both Jews and Gentiles alike.

Entry 14

During Paul's travels, the largest city on the Greek mainland was the city of Corinth. It boasted a population of well over half a million. It was situated near a small neck of land that separated the Aegean and Ionian Seas, thus making it an important point on the trade routes from the Middle East to Italy. Of the many industries of this commercial center, the pottery trade was well established and widely known.

Pottery was used for water pots, storage jars, cups and bowls, cooking utensils, lamps, ovens, and even toys for children. The pottery of Corinth was not only utilitarian, but it was also decorative, approaching the level of art.

Paul, as a tentmaker, was a man who worked with his hands. Surely he admired the hands of the potters as they molded lumps of clay into urns of magnificent beauty. In order for the clay to be molded and shaped, it needed to be pliable in the hands of the potter.

To be molded by God,
it is necessary for us to yield our wills
to the hands of the Potter.

The Potter's Hands

Acts 18

Based on Paul's stay in Corinth on his second journey.

Stopping in the potters' quarters,
*   I watched dried, cracked hands*
*   take chunks of crude clay and*
*   form them into wares for use.*
How useless is this clay while still in the earth.

Farmers lament its presence—
*   poor drainage*
*   infertile*
*   difficult,*
*   if not impossible, to plow.*

Yet, excavated from the earth,
*   put into the hands of the potter*
*   fashioned*
*   formed*
*   shaped*
*   molded*
Its uses are beyond number;
*   lamps for light*
*   vessels for drinking*
*   kettles for cooking*
*   urns for storage.*
Such utility!
And such beauty!
The vases of Corinth fill the earth;
*   their reputation is known by all.*

Decorated by the craftsman's hands
*   geometrical patterns of red and black*
*   floral patterns of vines and fields.*

Mere clay becomes a work of art.
As the prophet has written:
> **"Yet, O Lord, you are our Father.**
> **We are the clay, you are the potter;**
> **We are all the work of your hand."**
>
> Isaiah 64:8

Prayer

God of all creation
    mold me
    shape me
    into your vessel of service.   Jeremiah 18:6
Use me to do your will.

God of all creation,
    when others see my life
    may they see your beauty. . .
    the workmanship of your hand
        created in Christ Jesus.

Ephesians 2:10

Amen.

Historical Highlight
Greek Pottery

Ceramics: keramikos = "made of clay"

Paul mentions pottery in Romans 9:21-22; II Corinthians 4:7; I Thessalonians 4:4; II Timothy 2:21.

With its soil rich in clay, the Greeks developed many forms of ceramic pottery. Mainland Greece boasted of a high-quality clay which when fired turned to a reddish-brown color. Potters shaped wet clay on a potter's wheel and fired it in a kiln heated to about 1,000 degrees. Not only did the fire bake the pots, it also set any glazes or paints applied to the pots. Ceramic pieces played a large role in both trade and daily life.

Geometric Period: (circa 900 - 700 B.C.)
> Primarily geometric shapes painted in black against a background of tan or light yellow.

Protocorinthian Style: (730 - 625 B.C.)

Corinthian Style: (625 - 550 B.C.)
> Both styles primarily depict human or animal scenes amid floral decorations. A wider use of color and detail emerges.

Athenian Black-Figure Style: (600 - 520 B.C.)
> Primarily scenes from mythology; later scenes from daily life. Figures appear in black. Incisions create greater detail and finer lines.

Athenian Red-Figure Style: (520 - 400 B.C.)
> Red figures reverse the black figure technique. Figures were left open to the color of the clay while the background was fired black. Greater precision in detail.

Entry 15

The Olympic Games are remnants of the athletic games of ancient Greece that were held every four years in the city of Olympia. The Greeks highly valued sporting competitions, and they hosted four major athletic festivals that attracted competitors from all over the Greek world. One such festival was held at the Isthmus of Corinth in honor of Poseidon.

The athletes competed in a variety of contests including the pentathlon consisting of the long-jump, running, throwing the discus and the javelin, and wrestling. The athletes exercised in the gymnasium, training their bodies and minds to perform at peak levels.

Paul noted similarities between the disciplined life of the athlete and the life of a disciple of Christ. Both required determination and dedication. Both required desire and drive. But one was of temporary value, the other's value covered eternity. One resulted in a crown of leaves, the other in a crown of righteousness.

It's important to remember that
certain rewards are not worthy of the race.
Run for the gold!
Run for eternity!

Running the Race

Acts 18 and I Corinthians 9:24-27
Based on Paul's stay in Corinth on his second journey.

The athletic contests,
*   here at the Isthmus of Corinth,*
*   rival those of Olympia.*

From the corners of the earth
come all who seek to win the prize!

Wherever I look, men are in training:
The body is brought into harness,
Each muscle is challenged to its limit;
Sweat pours from the brow,
Determination is written on each face.

I Corinthians 9:24-27

The athlete's life demands
*   drive*
*   desire*
*   discipline*
*   dedication*
*   determination.*

Do any athletes train for second place!
*   By no means!*
They possess focus. . .
*   Yet, for what?*

*   The victor's crown*
*   of laurel leaves*
*   that wither at noon*
*   in the Peloponnese.*

Prayer

God of goodness and grace,

> *Give me the heart of an athlete,*
> *determined and disciplined to win!*

Yet, not for a mere prize
> *that is here today and gone tomorrow,*
But for the enduring prize. . .
> *Your crown of righteousness,*
> > *which you,*
> > *the Lord,*
> > *the righteous Judge,*
> > *will award to me on that day;*

And not only to me,
> *but to all who have longed*
> *for your appearing.*

> *May I run the race,*
> *May I keep the faith,*
> *May I win your prize.*
> > II Timothy 4:8

Glory be to you forever and ever.

> > *Amen.*

Historical Highlight
The Olympic Games

The Olympic Games were the oldest and most important of the ancient Greek sports-and-religious festivals. The earliest reliable date for the first Olympic Games is 776 B.C. although the Games began well before this date.

In the earliest years, the contests took place over the course of a day and included but two events: wrestling and a foot-race the length of the stadium. As the Games grew in popularity other contests were included: the pankration, meaning "total strength" or "complete victory," (wrestling/ boxing), chariot racing, and the pentathlon consisting of running, jumping, spear throwing, discus throwing, and wrestling. The winners of the events received nothing more than a garland of leaves.

The games remained prestigious through the Roman period. In A.D. 393 the Byzantine emperor, Theodosius I, ended the Games due to their pagan connotations.

Entry 16

Everyone involved in ministry to others needs a support system —close friends to call upon in times of need. The Apostle Paul found his support team in a wonderful couple, Prisca and Aquila. When the Roman Emperor, Claudius, ordered all the Jews to leave Rome, Prisca and Aquila were among those who left the city and re-located in Corinth. They, like Paul, were tentmakers. They, like Paul, shared a love for the Lord. So, the three of them lived and worked together. When Paul left Corinth, they joined him in his journey to Ephesus, where they set up their home.

Was it from this couple that Paul observed mutual respect and submission? Was the picture of this couple in his mind when he wrote to the husbands and wives in the church at Ephesus? "Look at the submission Prisca demonstrates toward her husband. And marvel at the love Aquila lavishes upon his wife. Their relationship is a reflection of the relationship between the Church and Christ."

Did they learn the secret of relationships from their trade? The needle needs the thread, the thread the needle. Each has a unique and valuable function. Working alone, nothing is accomplished. Joining together, they fulfill their purposes.

Submission and love are the thread
and needle of relationships.

A Remarkable Couple
Acts 18:1-3 and Ephesians 4
Based on Paul's relationship with Prisca and Aquila.

Today I met a remarkable couple!
Prisca and Aquila!

Like me, they have recently arrived in Corinth, though they
came from Rome.
> *(Claudius has ordered all the Jews*
> *to leave the imperial city.)*

We not only share the same trade as tent-makers, we also share
a common faith in Jesus Christ!

I am amazed at their relationship!
Out of reverence for Christ,
> *they submit to one another;*
>> *there are no demands placed on the other,*
>>> *there is no claiming of one's rights,*
>>> *there is no petty persistence of privilege.*

What I see in them is a spirit of gentleness,
> *an attitude of complete humility,*
> *a sensitivity toward the other person,*

And patience!
Working together, side by side,
> *they bear with one another in love.*
The bond between them is a bond of peace;
> *there is unity between their spirits!*

Ephesians 4:2-4

And how they speak to one another;
> *there is no unwholesome talk coming from their mouths,*
> *they say only what is helpful in building up the other!*

When I spoke with them,
inquiring about their life journey together,
they said that long ago
they mutually decided to put away
    all bitterness, rage, and anger!
    (such feelings only led to destroy relationships!)

Aquila said that at the foundation of their relationship was the
spirit of Christ—
        who was kind
        and compassionate to all,
        forgiving of others.

When they first heard and received the Gospel,
    they were overwhelmed by the forgiveness of Christ.
It was their desire to forgive one another
    just as they had been forgiven!

I liked how they said it. . .
    "We want to be imitators of God,
        living a life of love,
        just as Christ loved us
        and gave himself for us
        as a fragrant offering
        and sacrifice to God."
                Ephesians 5:1

    "As Christ loves us,
we are to love one another!"

Prisca and Aquila!
    Out of reverence for Christ,
    you submit to one another in love!

Prayer

Gracious God,

I thank you for Prisca and Aquila!
Bless their relationship which serves
    as a testimony to your love!

   May their days together
       bring happiness and joy;
   May their days together
       bear witness to your grace!
   May the same quality of the relationship
       between Prisca and Aquila
       be found in all my relationships, too.

Give me the mind of Christ
    the heart of Christ
    the patience of Christ
    the compassion of Christ

As I have been forgiven in Christ
may I forgive in a spirit of humility and gentleness,
bearing with others in love. . .
especially those dearest to me!

Let me imitate you!

Amen.

Tentmaker:

Luke states that Paul was a "tentmaker" (Acts 18:3), a weaver of tent cloth from goats' hair. The term can also mean one who was a leatherworker.

- It was not unusual for many rabbis to practice a trade. This was done so they might offer their teaching without a fee. Paul followed this procedure in his missionary activities; "These hands of mine have supplied my own needs and the needs of my companions" (Acts 20:34).

- By engaging in a trade he was able to set an example for his converts; "For you yourselves know how you ought to follow our example. We were not idle when we were with you, nor did we eat anyone's food without paying for it. On the contrary, we worked night and day, laboring and toiling so that we would not be a burden to any of you...For when we were with you, we gave you this rule: If a man will not work, he shall not eat" (II Thessalonians 3:7-10).

- By working, Paul was also able to avoid any criticism from his distracters who might accuse him of mercenary motives. Of course, when Paul was offered the hospitality of others, he received it in the same gracious manner in which it was offered.

Entry 17

Within the city of Corinth there was a sanctuary dedicated to the god, Asclepius, the Greek deity of healing. Those entering his sanctuary purified themselves with sacred waters, presented their sacrifices, offered a small gift, and then spent the night within the sanctuary. It was during the night the pilgrim received a dream from Asclepius. In the dream the patient was either cured or instructed as to the proper means to effect a cure. Upon awakening the person was to offer a gift which usually consisted of a work of art, or an inscription commemorating the cure. Often a reproduction in stone of the part of the body that was healed was presented, i.e., a foot, a leg, a hand.

Paul wrote his letter to the Romans while in Corinth. In this letter, he challenged Christians to present gifts to God. They were to offer, not inanimate objects, but their lives as "living sacrifices, holy and pleasing to God—which is genuine spiritual worship."

Jesus, the Lord of life,
desires we daily offer our everyday life to God.

Present Yourself

Romans 12:1 and 2
Based on Paul's view of pagan sacrifices.

Passing by the Temple of Asclepius
*   (the god of healing)*
I witnessed many entering the temple
*   carrying sculptured body parts,*
*   carvings of stone. . .*
*   hands, feet, ears, legs, arms. . .*

These pieces of stone are offered as votive offerings;
*   offerings of gratitude,*
*   offerings of devotion.*
Pieces of stones presented to a god portrayed in stone!
The idiocy of idolatry!

Yet, so often,
I am no different than these pagan pilgrims!
I present to God but a pretense of praise
*   from my heart of stone.*
I seek to satisfy my God with a small token of
*   appreciation.*

*   "Accept, O God, my foot,*
*   Accept, O God, my arm.*
*   Accept, O God,*
*   but a moment of my time,*
*   a small portion of my life."*

How foolish I am! God desires all of me—
*   completely, wholly.*
In view of God's mercy toward me,
how can I give Him less!

I am to present to the Giver of life all my life—
my every move, my every moment,
my every breath, my every belief,
my every act, my every attitude,
my every task, my every talent,
my every day, my every night,
my every hour, my every minute;

For my life is not my own!
I was bought with a price,
the precious blood of Christ,
the one who died for me
so that I might live for Him!

This is to be my spiritual act of worship:
This is the gift that pleases my God.

Prayer

Merciful God,

May I not conform to the ways of this world;
May I not seek to appease you with a token offering,
or with a pitiful portion,
or with a half-hearted commitment.
Take all of me! I sacrifice my life to You;

For from You and through You
and to You are all things!   Romans 11:36

Break my heart of stone;
Make me Yours alone!
To You be glory forever.

Amen.

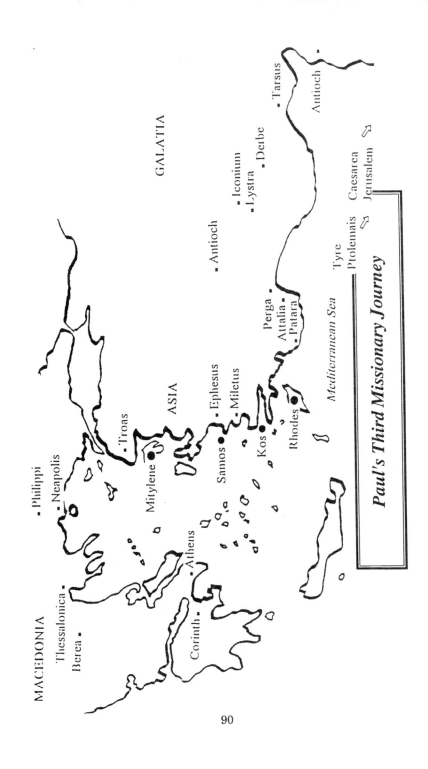

Paul's Third Missionary Journey

MACEDONIA
GALATIA
ASIA

Philippi
Neapolis
Thessalonica
Berea
Troas
Mitylene
Athens
Corinth
Samos
Ephesus
Miletus
Kos
Rhodes
Antioch
Perga
Attalia
Patara
Iconium
Lystra
Derbe
Tarsus
Antioch
Tyre
Ptolemais
Caesarea
Jerusalem

Mediterranean Sea

Entry 18

The olive, the vineyard, grain and sheep were the basis of the agricultural economy of the Mediterranean world. Many of Jesus' parables dealt with such topics: the sower and the seeds, the wheat and weeds, the workers in the vineyard, the lost sheep. When Jesus sent out his appointed disciples, he spoke of their mission in agricultural terms,

> *"The harvest is plentiful, but the workers are few.*
> *Ask the Lord of the harvest, therefore,*
> *to send out workers into his harvest field..."*
> Luke 10:2

Paul also drew upon the world of farming. He spoke of himself as one called to plant the seed of the Gospel. He called upon the Christian community to produce fruit to God. He described the work of the Holy Spirit as yielding fruit in the life of the believer. Paul also looked forward to the time of harvest—the day of Christ's coming. On that day, those who sowed seeds of righteousness would reap the joy of eternal life.

Jesus and Paul stated what all farmers know—
a tree is known by its fruit and what is sown bears forth a harvest.

The Harvest

Galatians 5 and 6
Based on Paul's travels through
the plains of Asia Minor.

Everywhere I look the fields glisten with golden shafts of grain
swaying in the breeze.

The harvest is being gathered.
The fields now yield their fruits.
The farmers' efforts of planting, and tending,
*   and pruning,*
*   and cultivating,*
*   now culminate in the abundance of the harvest!*

The seeds planted in the springtime
*   now yield their autumn crop. . .*
*   wheat and barley,*
*   oats and rye.*
The cycle is complete.
What was sown is reaped!
As the earthly cycle moves from sowing to reaping,
so also the spiritual cycle!

The harvest is coming soon!
Those seeds sown to please the sinful nature. .
*   immorality, impurity,*
*   debauchery, idolatry,*
*   witchcraft,*
*   hatred, discord,*
*   jealousy, fits of rage,*
*   selfish ambition,*
*   factions, dissension, envy,*
*   drunkenness,*
*   orgies and the like,*
*   will produce a harvest of destruction!*

We must not be deceived,
God cannot be mocked:
Those who sow such seeds
will not enter into the kingdom of God!

Prayer

O God, of the harvest
the day of Christ's return is at hand.
May I be found to have sown seeds pleasing to your Spirit. . .
joy
love
peace
kindness
goodness
gentleness
faithfulness
self-control.

May I live by the Spirit;
May I keep in step with the Spirit.
May I never grow weary in doing well!
May I reap eternal life.

In the name of the Lord Jesus Christ,
who gave himself for my sins to rescue me
from the present evil age,
according to the will of God the Father,
to whom be glory
for ever and ever.
Galatians 1:3-5

Amen.

Historical Highlight
Farming and The Olive Tree

The farms of Greece primarily grew grains, olives and grapes (used in the making of wine). Of the grains, barley was the most common with wheat often imported from Ukraine and Sicily. By the fifth century B.C., the Greek farmer practiced the annual rotation of crops. Plowing and seeding generally occurred in October. Plows were wooden rigs pulled behind a pair of yoked oxen.

Due to the mountainous terrain of mainland Greece, one of the predominant crops for cultivation was the olive tree. The oil of the olive was used in a variety of ways: cooking, washing, lamp fuel, and religious ceremonies. It also played an important role in commerce as a leading product for exportation.

In Greek mythology, Athena was credited as the one responsible for the introduction of the olive tree to the citizens of Athens. The legend said that Athena and Poseidon argued over who would become the patron deity of Athens. The gods engaged in a contest to see which one of them could offer the best gift to the citizens of this noble city. The contest took place on the summit of the acropolis. Poseidon struck the ground with his trident resulting in a salt water spring. Athena struck the ground with her spear and from the spot there sprouted the first olive tree. The citizens awarded Athena the position of overseer of Athens.

Entry 19

Heralding the coming of the Messiah, John the Baptist proclaimed the message of the prophet Isaiah:

> *Make straight a highway for our God. Every valley shall be raised up, every mountain and hill made low; the rough ground shall become level, the rugged places a plain.*
> Isaiah 40:3b-4

Was John reminded of this prophecy by the sight of the numerous Roman roads being construction throughout the land of Israel? After all, the Romans were masters road builders. Their highways stretched from the banks of the Euphrates to the boundaries of Britain. By the end of the third century A.D., their network covered over 50,000 miles. One Roman historian, Plutarch, wrote:

> *"The roads were carried through the country in a perfectly straight line, and were paved with hewn stone and reinforced with banks of tight-rammed sand. Depressions were filled up, all intersecting torrents or ravines were bridged, and both sides were of equal and corresponding height, so that the work presented everywhere an even and beautiful appearance."*

Paul knew much about roads. He walked from city to city, covering thousands of miles—sometimes on the level highways of the Romans, sometimes on unpaved mountain tracks. The quality of the roads dictated the distance of his daily progress. Good roads made for good travel.

The paths we choose in our pilgrimage
to God set the pace of our own spiritual progress.
The secret is to stay off dead end roads!

Walk in the Way

Colossians 3:7
Based on the Highways of Paul's Travels.

Sand, rock, gravel,
Pick, shovel, hoe.
Dust flying everywhere!
Stones hewn and chiseled;

Valleys filled with rubble,
Hills brought down low;
Rough ground made level,
Rugged places flattened into a plain.

As we traveled today,
we watched the Romans bustling about
        as road construction was underway;
        such monumental works performed
        with energy and expertise.

How brilliant they are in their labor,
How well planned are their routes;
        No unnecessary turns,
        No wasted bends;

                Each step planned,
                Every mile measured.

They know where they want to go
        and the best means to get there;
        no detours, and no dead ends.

I wish this could be said of those who journey on the path of
God!

Yet, today I received word from Epaphras that some of those in
Colosse have strayed from the path which leads to godliness.

They are walking in the way of the world,
parading down dead end streets they formerly knew.
Colossians 3:7

What heartache!

The road they are constructing
 leads only to their destruction!
The path they travel is riddled with ruts and ditches. . .
 ruts of ruin and ditches of doom.
On such a path they will never find the kingdom of God.
I Corinthians 15:34

How quickly they have forgotten
 that the way to God leads to life,
  while the way of the wicked leads to death.

I have written them, urging them to come back to their senses.

The road sign of God reads,

"Stop Sinning!"
I Corinthians 15:34

So wise are the words of Solomon
when he offered guidance for godliness. . .

"Flee the path of the wicked
and walk not in the way of evil.
Avoid it, do not travel on it
turn from it and go on your way.

Make level paths for your feet
and take only ways that are firm.
Do not swerve to the right or the left;
keep your foot from evil."
Proverbs 4:14-15, 26-27

Prayer

Lord of life,
Your word is a lamp to my feet
and a light for my path.
Guard my steps and illumine the way before me.

When I wander from Your way,
put me once again on the path to life.
When I stumble and fall,
pick me up and set me straight.
When I march headlong down dead end roads,
turn me around and redirect my steps.

With a heart full of sorrow,
I lift up before you those who have strayed down the highway
of destruction;

Show them Your warning sign,
and the folly of their course,
the wickedness of their ways;
and the ruin awaiting them at their destination.

Lead them again in paths of righteousness
and restore within them a right spirit.
Keep my heart on the right path
so I may enter Your gates with thanksgiving
and Your courts with praise.

Your love, O Lord, is good and endures forever.
Your faithfulness continues through all generations.
Psalm 100:4
Your path leads me to life everlasting.

Praise be to the name of Jesus Christ,
who is the truth and the life and the way.
John 14:6

Amen.

Entry 20

Life is ever transforming...simply watch a child grow up—a young gangly girl develops into a graceful ballerina; an awkward boy becomes a superb athlete; a timid student goes into politics; a mischievous child serves as a missionary!

Transformation is at the heart of the Good News! The word Paul uses for transformation is ***metamorphousthai.*** This word means more than a mere change on the surface, more that a change in external appearances. It is the change of a person's inner being, the change of a person's heart. Paul knew such a transformation. His life was a living witness to such power. He described it as

> *"being crucified with Christ and no longer living,*
> *but Christ living within..."*
> Galatians 2:20

After concluding his third missionary journey, Paul set sail to Jerusalem. Along the way, he visited several islands, among them Rhodes. This island with its numerous butterflies was also called "Butterfly Island." How appropriate it is that Paul visited this land of the caterpillar/butterfly!

Out of God's treasury,
we are given the generous gift of transformation.
God makes all things new!

A New Creation

Acts 21:1

Based on Paul's stay in Rhodes on his third journey.

Rhodes. . .
an island paradise,
beauty and sunlight abound.
> *(Because of our arduous pace, Luke admonished us*
> *to get some rest. . .good advice from a loving and*
> *caring physician!)*

Our pace has been grueling,
> *with many more days of sailing still ahead;*
> *to Tyre, landing at Ptolemais,*
> *setting sail again for Caesarea.*
While there, we hope to stay at the home of Philip, the evange-
list. Then on to Jerusalem!

Young Timothy urged us to accompany him to Petaloudes, the
valley of butterflies located on this island. He has heard that the
vanilla-scented resin of this valley's storax trees attracts thou-
sands of butterflies. They are called "quadrina" from four spots
and a Roman numeral IV on each wing. In flight their wings
open out in a flutter of black, brown, white and red.

Timothy was amazed and filled with great delight.
He is so full of joy and laughter.
My true son!

II Timothy 1:2

Butterflies everywhere!
One even landed on my bald head.
We all laughed.
It has been a good day for us.

Butterflies everywhere!
  remarkable creatures!
  from ugly, crawling caterpillars
  to glorious, spectacles of flight!

Transformed by God's creative hand;
  the same hand that took this ugly,
  crawling sinner and clothed him
    in the righteousness of Christ!

  If anyone is in Christ,
    There is a new creation!
    the old is gone,
    the new has come!
      II Corinthians 5:17

Prayer

Gracious God,
Thank you for the delights of this day
  laughter with good and dear friends
  the beauty of creation
  and butterflies!

Above all, I thank you for transforming me,
    a sinner
    saved by grace!
      Ephesians 2:5

In return, may I live
  for you who died for me
    and you were raised again!
      II Corinthians 5:15

  Amen.

In the second century B.C., Philo of Byzantium wrote a work entitled *Concerning the Seven Wonders of the World.* In this work he listed what were considered by the Greek and Roman world of his time, the greatest feats of human design.

I. The Pyramids of Egypt

All but one of the Seven Wonders has been destroyed by either the passage of time or the destruction of humankind. The Pyramids of Egypt stand today as a monumental testimony to the great pharaohs of the past. The largest pyramid is the Great Pyramid of Khufu (Cheops), rising about 482 feet high on a base of 755 feet square.

II. The Hanging Gardens of Babylon

Legend said that Nebuchadnezzar II (c. 605-562) built the terraced gardens around his palace so his wife, Mede, might have a reminder of her mountainous homeland.

III. The Temple of Artemis at Ephesus

This Greek temple was built c. 560 B.C. and dedicated to the patron deity of the city, the goddess Artemis (Diana). During Paul's visit to Ephesus, his message convinced many people to turn away from the worship of Artemis. This resulted in a furious riot instigated by the silversmiths who made their living by making silver shrines dedicated to the goddess (Acts 19).

IV. The Statue of Zeus at Olympia

Within the temple of Olympia and sitting upon an elaborate throne adorned with ebony, glass and gemstone inlays was the god, Zeus (436-432 B.C.). Even while seated, the statue nearly touched the ceiling. When in Lystra, **Barnabas** and **Paul** healed a crippled man. When the citizens saw this, they praised Barnabas as the Greek god Zeus and Paul as Hermes, the chief messenger of the gods (Acts 14).

V. The Mausoleum at Halicarnassus
This monument has given its name to all subsequent tomb monuments. Mausolus, satrap of Caria, was presented with this tomb by his Queen, Artemisia (350 B.C.)

VI. The Colossus of Rhodes
The Colossus of Rhodes was erected as a thank offering to the Greek god, Helios. Made of bronze and erected in the third century B.C., the statue was of the young god, wearing a sun-ray crown and gazing out to sea. He stood approximately 120' high on a platform of white marble 20-25'. After standing majestically over the city of Rhodes for 60 years, it broke at the knees and toppled to the ground during an earthquake. With the Arab invasion of 653 A.D., it was dismantled and sold for scrap metal. Paul stopped at Rhodes in his final sea journey to Jerusalem (Acts 21).

VII. The Pharos of Alexandria.
The Pharos (284-280 B.C.) served as the prototype for ancient lighthouses. It was dedicated to the 'savior gods' on behalf of all sailors. The tower stood 400 feet high in which either resinous wood or oil was kept burning. The light from the flame, visible for up to 30 miles, was reflected by metal mirrors.

Entry 21

During Paul's first missionary journey, a young man named Timothy, along with his mother Eunice and grandmother Lois, became a follower of Christ. Timothy's father, a Gentile, had passed away; when, we are uncertain, but probably while Timothy was a child. Regardless of the exact date, we know that Timothy's religious training was conducted by his grandmother and mother who were Jews. While he was but an infant, they began to instruct him in the holy Scriptures—teaching, correcting, rebuking, and training Timothy in the righteousness of God. It was through their loving efforts that Timothy developed a sincere faith in God.

When Paul reasoned from the Scriptures with this family, they accepted his message and received Jesus as the fulfillment of the Old Testament. Timothy's faith in Christ grew and grew. During his second campaign, Paul asked Timothy to join his missionary team. Through their years of ministry together, their relationship grew stronger and deeper. In fact, Paul called Timothy his "true son." As the years passed, Timothy took on greater leadership responsibilities within the Church, faithfully preaching the Word of God.

Thanks is due to the mother and grandmother of Timothy. They recognized the importance of feasting upon God's Word.

The Word of God is sweeter than honey in the honeycomb; more precious than the purest gold!

God's Maternal Gift

II Timothy 1:5
Based on Paul's second letter to Timothy.

Dear Lois and Eunice,
Greetings in the name of Jesus Christ!

Every time I see the faith of young Timothy,
my heart is filled with the remembrance of you.
Let no one underestimate the value of mothers
and grandmothers!

It was through your prayers and godly lives that Timothy
was shown the way of Christ.
From infancy, you took Tim upon your lap and taught him
the Word of God.

You impressed upon his heart
the value of heeding the Scriptures
which have made him
wise for salvation
through faith in Jesus Christ.
II Timothy 3:15

You breathed into his life the very breath of God
that gives life to all.
Through the Word,
you taught,
rebuked,
corrected and
trained him in righteousness.

Now he is equipped for every good work as a man of God!
II Timothy 3:16 and 17

You have prepared him
to preach the Word
to keep his head in all situations
to endure hardships
to do the work of an evangelist
and to carry out a dynamic ministry for Christ!
II Timothy 4:1,5

Daily, I thank God for the two of you,
constantly remembering you in my prayers.

Prayer

Gracious God,

For Lois and Eunice, I give You thanks.
May others see their example and seek to serve You as they have
served You.

Give them, and all parents and grandparents,
the strength, the wisdom, the patience,
and the love and joy of Christ!
Let their lives fan into flame,
in their children and grandchildren,
a burning desire to know You and to trust in You.
II Timothy 1:6

Now to the King eternal,
immortal,
invisible,
the only God,
be honor and glory
for ever and ever.
I Timothy 1:17

Amen.

Entry 22

Paul preached the message of Christ and him crucified. As he proclaimed the message of the cross, he was well aware of the words of Jesus,

> *"If any man would come after me,*
> *he must deny himself*
> *and take up his cross daily and follow me."*
> Luke 9:23

For Paul, he was not only called to believe in Christ but also to suffer for Him. As he suffered, he in some strange way shared in the very suffering of Christ, the very work of Christ. And if he shared in Christ's sufferings, he knew he would also share in Christ's glory, and the power of the resurrection. Suffering was by no means a penalty but a privilege!

Paul suffered greatly at the hands of many. At times he was near to death. Yet when he thought of the eternal glory awaiting him, he viewed the tribulations of the day as "light and momentary troubles."

We are called to share Christ's cross,
Christ's death,
Christ's resurrection,
Christ's life forevermore!

To Suffer for You
Acts 14:19; 16:22
Based on the numerous beatings that Paul endured.

Frequently imprisoned,
  flogged severely,
  exposed to death again and again,
  five times whipped forty lashes minus one,
  three times beaten with rods,
  once beaten with stones,
  three times shipwrecked,
  one night and day in the open sea;
    in danger from rivers,
    in danger from bandits,
    in danger from my own countrymen,
    in danger from Gentiles,
    in danger in the city,
    in danger in the country,
    in danger at sea,
    in danger from false brothers;
labored and toiled often without sleep,
knowing hunger and thirst;
cold and naked...

II Corinthians 11:25-27

I am hard pressed on every side,
  but not crushed;
  perplexed,
  but not abandoned;
  struck down,
  but not destroyed.

II Corinthians 4:8-9

I bear on my body the marks of Jesus;

Galatians 6:17

I carry around in my body the death of Jesus!

110

Outwardly I am wasting away,
but
my spirit is being renewed daily;

This mortal body is dying,
but my spirit is overflowing with joy;
Death is at work within me,
but my spirit is filled with the life of Christ.

Battered, pressed down on every side,
Tossed about by the raging tide;
Beaten and bruised, who hears my cry?
Then I remember, Lord, how you died!

Left, abandoned by my foes,
Flogged, smitten, and struck down low;
Accursed, despised, does no one know?
Then I remember your blood that flowed!

Whipped by the lash upon my back,
How many the times I've been attacked;
Shall I give up, retreat, fall back?
Then I remember when the sky turned black!

Lord, your suffering is mine too!
I'll endure the pain as I live for you.
When I survey my heart's renewed,
So keep your cross within my view!

Prayer

Father of compassion, God of all comfort,
on your behalf,
grant me not only to believe in you,
but also to suffer for you.
Philippians 1:29

For as I share in your suffering,
I know that I shall also share in your splendor!

Compared with the glory that will be revealed in me,
I can endure the present tribulations of this
world as if they were nothing.
                    Romans 8:17-18

In those moments of life
    moments of despair
    moments of trial
    moments of failing endurance,
    moments when I am tempted to give up or give in,
    teach me anew that my strength is in you. . .
        my Hope, my Deliverer, my Comfort!

This is my prayer,
in the name of the one who endured all for my sake!

My Sacrifice
and
My Savior.

Amen.

Entry 23

The Roman Empire was the dominant political and military might in the first century world of the New Testament. The only protection an individual possessed against her arbitrary use of force was to be a Roman citizen. All others within the empire must fear her hand.

Citizenship provided three primary benefits:
- citizens were exempted from torture or corporal punishment without a trial;
- they were subject only to the laws of Rome and not those of other lands;
- they could present legal disputes before the imperial court.

Paul was born a Roman citizen; thus, his father must have possessed this privilege. How his father, a Jew, received this citizenship is not known. Perhaps it was granted to him because of some service he rendered to the state. Or perhaps an influential friend secured it for him from the emperor. On occasions, Paul claimed the rights of citizenship. It was because of it that he was able to appeal his legal case to Caesar, which eventually brought him to Rome.

Roman citizenship was a prized possession, but for Paul it paled in significance to his citizenship in the kingdom of God.

Our citizenship is in heaven where Christ reigns
as the
King of kings
and the Lord of lords.

A Citizen of Heaven
Acts 22:22-29
Based on Paul's arrest in Jerusalem.

With my hands bound by chains
and my back stripped bare. . .
With the whip of leather
weighted with pieces of metal and bone,
set and ready to strike. . .
With the soldiers breathing out their threats,
uttering vile insults and epithets. . .
I need only to make one claim, and with it,
everything comes to a halt!

"Ciuis Romannus sum!
I am a Roman citizen!"
Acts 22:25

What power is found in these words;
the guards are stunned
they dropped to their knees in fear
they quickly unfettered my chains
The alert is dispatched. . .
"Find the commander; relay the news.
Do not delay; report his claim"

They understand, too fully,
that any violation of a Roman's rights
invites the wrath of Roman retribution!

Such a powerful empire;
no one dares question her authority
no one dares question her might.
She deals swiftly with those who defy her decrees.
Rome equals authority and power.
no mercy,
no leniency.

114

And yet, one day, this claim,
>>*"I am a citizen of Rome"*
>*will bear no weight. . .*

This empire, like all empires before her,
>*will be no more!*
Fading into the past,
>*her power will wane and cease.*

There is only one empire
>*that shall endure the passage of time;*
>>*only one empire that shall not wane in power. . .*
>>*only one empire that shall last forever. . .*
>*And of this empire, I am a citizen!*
>>>>Philippians 3:20

Prayer

>>>*God,*
>>*the blessed and only Ruler,*
>>*the King of kings and Lord of lords,*
>>>*who alone is immortal*
>>*and who lives in unapproachable light,*
>>*whom no one has seen or can see:*
>>*May all honor and might be yours forever.*
>>>I Timothy 6:15 and 16

>>*That my citizenship is in heaven,*
>>>*I give you thanks!*
>>*I eagerly long for the day of Christ's coming,*
>*the day when all creation will be under his control,*
>>*the day when he will transform*
>>>*this lowly body of mine*
>>>*into a glorious body.*
>>>*Until that day,*
>>*may I stand firm for you.*

>>>*Amen.*

Gallio: During Paul's time in the city of Corinth, Gallio was the Roman proconsul of Achaea (lower Greece). The position of proconsul was granted to those who had held the highest office in Rome, the consulship. The Senate assigned proconsuls to administer the peaceful provinces of the empire. Gallio served in this capacity at Corinth around 52 A.D. When the leaders of the Jewish synagogue wanted to bring charges against Paul, they appeared before the tribunal of Gallio. He refused to hear their accusations and dismissed the case as nothing more than a mere squabble over the interpretations of religious regulations and words of theology. With such a ruling, Paul was able to continue his ministry in Corinth for some time. (Acts 18:12-17)

Felix: As a Roman official, Felix ruled as governor of Judea from about 53-60 A.D. His headquarters were located in Caesarea. The Jews, under the direction of the high priest Ananias and a lawyer named Tertullus, brought charges against Paul to Felix. For two years Felix held Paul under guard while allowing him some freedom as well as the company of his friends. Luke states that Felix was well acquainted with the Way, as the followers of Jesus were known. Paul spoke to Felix on numerous occasions, sharing with him God's call to faith in Jesus Christ. Felix left office in 60 A.D. probably under a purge initiated by the Emperor Nero. Upon leaving office and wanting to garner favor with the Jews, he turned Paul over to his successor, Porcius Festus. (Acts 24)

Festus: As Festus succeeded Felix, he, too, wanted to win the favor of the Jews. In response to the urging of the chief priests and the Jewish leaders, Festus reopened the case against Paul. Serious charges were brought against the apostle. Paul was perceptive enough to realize that such a hearing was stacked against him, so he appealed his case to Caesar which was his right as a Roman citizen. Festus responded by saying, "You have appealed to Caesar, so to Caesar you will go." (Acts 25)

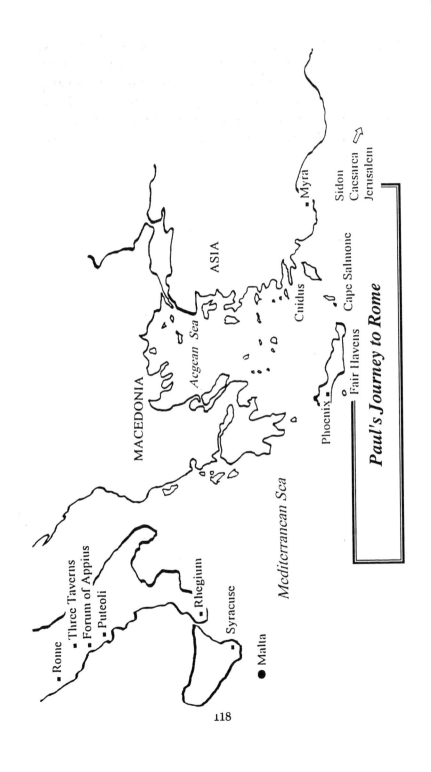

Paul's Journey to Rome

Rome
Three Taverns
Forum of Appius
Puteoli

Rhegium

Syracuse

Malta

Mediterranean Sea

MACEDONIA

Aegean Sea

ASIA

Phoenix

Fair Havens

Cnidus

Cape Salmone

Myra

Sidon
Caesarea
Jerusalem

Entry 24

While awaiting his trial in Rome, Paul was imprisoned. During this time he wrote the letter to the Ephesians. Whereas most of his letters were written while on the road and directed toward specific issues within the life of a particular Christian community, this letter was different. It was written without the urgency of a crisis or a brewing controversy. Paul now had time to be more reflective in his writing, resulting in a less didactic presentation.

This letter is lyrical and poetic. Someone has called it "a poem in prose." As it is read, we can hear the song of praise which overflowed from the heart of Paul. His inner being bursts forth with glad shouts of gratitude for the grace that had saved him, not based upon his works, but through faith in the Lord Jesus Christ.

The heart of gratitude sings the song of praise!

❖

"Then sings my soul,
my Savior God, to Thee,
How great Thou art,
How great Thou art!"

Hymn of Praise

Ephesians 1:1-23
Based on Paul's praise to God while imprisoned in Rome.

Praise be to the God and Father
of our Lord Jesus Christ;
Praise be to God who has blessed us
with every spiritual blessing.
Praise be to God who chose us in Christ
before the creation of the world.
Praise be to God who makes us
holy and blameless in His sight.

Praise be to God who lovingly adopts us
as His sons and daughters.
Praise be to God
who showers us with His glorious grace
who redeems us through the blood of Christ
who has forgiven us our sins
who has chosen us as His own
who has given us hope through Christ.

Praise be to God
for the word of truth
for the gospel of salvation
for the seal of the Holy Spirit
for the inheritance that shall be ours.

Praise be to God who brings all things
in heaven and on earth
under one head,
Christ Jesus, our Savior and Lord.

Praise be to God
for raising Christ from the dead

120

seating Christ at His right hand
giving Christ all rule and authority, power and dominion
placing all things under Christ's feet
appointing Christ to be head over everything
   for the church, which is Christ's body,
   and the fullness of God
   who fills everything in every way.

Prayer

Loving Father,
As my ministry draws to a close,
may Your praises be found on my lips
as I breathe my last breath.

Even now, my heart is filled with love
for Your Church—and so,
I kneel before You,
from whom the whole family in heaven
and on earth derives its name.

I pray that out of Your glorious riches,
You will strengthen Your people
with power through Your Spirit.

May Christ dwell in their hearts through faith;
Establish Your people in Your love
that surpasses knowledge;
Fill them with the measure of all the fullness of Christ.

Gracious God, You do immeasurably more
than all I can ask or imagine!
Glory be to Your Name, and the Name
of Christ Jesus through all generations,
for ever and ever.

Amen!

Entry 25

The authority of Rome stretched across a vast empire, extending from Britain to the Euphrates and from Germany to the coast of Africa. Throughout the provinces of the Empire, Roman might was displayed through its armies.

Paul encountered many soldiers during his days, especially centurions. They were the chief leaders in battle. They were the career soldiers who generally had risen through the ranks. In *Acts* several centurions are mentioned: the first Gentile convert was a centurion named Cornelius (Acts 10:22); when an assassination plot was uncovered against Paul, a centurion provided for Paul's safety (Acts 23:23); Felix, the Roman governor of Judea, ordered a centurion to guard Paul (Acts 24:23); during Paul's journey to Rome, when soldiers wanted to kill the prisoners who might escape during a shipwreck, a centurion saved Paul's life and the lives of others by reissuing orders (Acts 27:43).

The soldiers of Rome trusted in their armor. They carried with them an oblong shield, a short double-bladed sword, and wore a helmet that sometimes had a plume at the top. They also wore a kilt of leather or metal-plated strips. Battle engagement was often hand-to-hand combat. A soldier's armor was his last line of defense.

Paul knew himself to be engaged in combat. His adversary was the power of evil, the devil. The battles were fierce and frequently fought. Like the centurions of Rome, Paul trusted in his armor—armor forged and fitted by God.

Those engaged in combat know the value of their equipment
and the necessity of being prepared at all times.
When the battle cry is sounded there is no time for delay.

Stand Our Ground

Ephesians 6:10-20
Based upon Paul's role as an "Ambassador in Chains."

The sentry, posted outside my cell is dressed for battle;
As a member of the Roman royal guard,
    he stands at attention
    clad in the gear of war.

His tunic is held in place by a belt,
    allowing for maximum mobility.
His breastplate of bronze depicts the ridges of chest muscles so
    designed to deflect the enemy's blows.
His sandals are connected to greaves of metal wrapped around
    each lower leg to provide protection.
His shield is in hand. The most dangerous of weapons, the fiery
    dart (dipped in pitch and set aflame) would sink into its
    wooden center and thus be extinguished.
His helmet glistens from hours of polishing. Upon his head it sits
    like the crown of a king.
His sword has seen countless conflicts and slain soldiers too
    numerous to know.

Night and day, he stands prepared to engage the enemy.

He is vigilant. . .
    never diverting his gaze
    never forgetting his duty
    never compromising his mission.

Such preparations for battle
    against mere mortals of flesh and blood!

We, too, must be prepared for battle,
but against a far greater opponent
    of a very different sort.

We contend against the devil. . .
     the ruler of this dark world
     the spiritual force of evil in the heavenly realms.
He is unrivaled in crafty ruses as well as direct assault;
     his weapons of destruction are intimidation
     and insinuation.
He is like a raging wolf masked in sheep's clothing,
     looking for prey in which to sink his fangs.
He never slumbers nor sleeps.
He never surrenders nor retreats.
He never veers from his strategy—

His banner reads. . .
               "Death to all!"

This is our Adversary;
And against him we must stand our ground!

We must be strong in the Lord
     and in the mighty power of God.
We must put on the full armor of God
     so that we will not falter nor fail when assaulted.

And O, how remarkable is our armor.
It has not crafted by the hand of the metalworker.
It has been forged by the very hand of God!

Truth is the buckle around our waists.
Righteousness is our breastplate.
Peace is the leather upon our soles,
     durable for the march because the battle is long
     and the leather must last.
Faith is our shield protecting us
     from the fiery arrows hurled at us by our Antagonist.
Salvation is our helmet.

We are prepared for combat.
The Word of God is the sword
in our right hand
in our left we wield
the weapon of prayer!

We march into battle with the banner of God unfurled for all to see—

"Victory through our Lord Jesus Christ."
I Corinthians 15:57

The God of peace will soon crush Satan under our feet!
Romans 16:20

Prayer

Lord of power and might—
I am weak but You are strong
I am fearful but You are fearless.

Give me Your strength
so I may stand
against the powers
of evil and death.

Make me fearless
so I may hold my ground
against the sinister scheme's of Satan.

May I be strong in the grace that is in my Savior.
May I be faithful to my commanding officer.
II Timothy 2:4
May I endure hardship like a good soldier of Christ Jesus.
II Timothy 2:3

May I stand firm in the face of battle so that I may
  fearlessly make known the mystery of the gospel,
  for which I am an ambassador in chains.
                                        Ephesians 6:20

May my love for Christ Jesus be an undying love.
        May my service to Him
              be faithful
              and loyal
              and true.

Amen.

JULIUS CAESAR	Assassinated 44 BC - March 15
AUGUSTUS	27 BC - 14
TIBERIUS	14 - 37
CALIGULA	37 - 41
CLAUDIUS I	41 - 54
NERO	54 - 68
GALBA	68 - 69
OTHO	69
VITELLIUS	69
VESPASIAN	69 - 79
TITUS	75 - 81
DOMITIAN	81 - 96

In various passages, Paul wrote words of instruction concerning behavior towards those in the role of the government. He states that those in authority have been placed in their positions by the establishment of God. God has appointed them as protectors of the peace, those who maintain public order, and as the administrators of justice. Paul encouraged the Christian community to be subject to those in public office, remembering them in pray before God's throne (Romans 13:1-7; I Timothy 2:1-2; Titus 3:1).

Entry 26

During the ministry of Paul, there were many who served with him. The list is long and yet our information about most of them is limited. In Paul's letter to the Philippians, we learn of a fellow worker named Epaphroditus. He was from Philippi and was sent to assist Paul during his time of imprisonment in Rome. While with Paul, Epaphroditus became ill, nearly to the point of death (see Philippians 2). Paul sent him back home in order for him to regain his strength. Epaphroditus also carried with him the letter of Paul to the Philippians.

This reading speculates that Epaphroditus' health did not improve as hoped, and that his illness worsened, resulting in death. Perhaps it was such an event that prompted Paul to pen I Corinthians chapter fifteen—"the life yet to be."

Human sorrow finds its comfort
in the hope of God's heavenly home.

Every Tear

I Corinthians 15
Based upon Paul's friendship with Epaphroditus.

---

*Today a messenger arrived from Philippi with news that brings
me great sorrow...*

A dear friend,
   a brother,
   a fellow worker,
   and fellow soldier has died;
   and my heart is filled with an aching sadness!

Such a faithful servant of God!
Such a faithful friend of mine.
I miss him more than words can say.

He served the Lord with great joy!
Men such as he are worthy of honor!
Men such as he are worthy of praise!

On many occasions,
he risked his life for the work of Christ!

Philippians 2:25-30

And yet,
in the midst of my sorrow I can rejoice!

God raised Christ from the dead
   on the third day according to the Scriptures,
   appearing to Peter,
   and the Twelve,
   and to over 500 of the brothers at the same time,
   and James,
   then to all the apostles...
   and even to me,
      the least of the apostles
      who does not even deserve to be called an apostle...

130

but
by the grace of God I am what I am.
Christ was raised from the dead,
Christ is the Risen Lord!

His resurrection is
the guarantee for all who have fallen asleep,
*   the hope upon which we stake our lives,*
*   the proof of all that we believe. . .*
*   (if this is not so, we have no hope;*
*   we are to be pitied more than all of humanity.)*

This is the message of God upon
which I have taken my stand
and upon which I stake my life.

As the prophet Isaiah wrote:
"On this mountain
the Lord Almighty
will prepare a feast
of rich food for all peoples—
On this mountain
the Lord Almighty
will destroy the shroud
that enfolds all peoples,
the sheet that covers all;
The Lord will swallow up death forever.
The Sovereign Lord will wipe away
the tears from their faces."
Isaiah 25:6-8

"Where, O death, is your victory?
Where, O death, is your sting?"
Hosea 13:14

My tears flow because of my loss—
*   but they are dried*
*   by the victory of Christ!*

131

My tears flow because of my love—
but they are wiped away
by the very hand of God!

Prayer

Gracious God,
Throughout my life, You are with me!
From the day of my birth until
the night of my death,
You hold me in Your hand.

Even when facing the grave,
I see Your face and I have no fear
for Your face is the face of the Risen Christ!
Guard my heart from the gloom of grieving
like people without hope,
for You are my hope!
With the coming resurrection,
You shall clothe me in splendor!

Until that day,
may I give myself fully to Your work,
for I know that my labor
for You is never in vain!

Thanks be to You,
O God and
Christ our Lord,
who triumphed over death,
who reigns as the Victor
upon the throne
for ever and ever!

Come, O Lord!
I Corinthians 16:22

Amen.

Entry 27

Paul's great desire for the church was unity. The society surrounding her was full of divisions—divisions between the wealthy few and the poor masses, patricians and plebeians, masters and slaves, Gentiles and Jews, Greeks and barbarians, males and females.

The Gospel came to destroy such divisions. No longer could the educated Greek look down upon the uneducated barbarian. Both possessed the wisdom of God's Spirit. No longer could the ceremonial clean call unclean those whom God had purified through Christ. No longer could the master classify a slave as nothing more than merely a living tool. In Christ, both master and slave were debtors to grace. Labels such as barbarian, unclean, slave—were replaced by the words brother and sister.

Most of Paul's letters were written to communities. On occasion he did pen personal pages. One such letter was sent to Philemon, a slave owner. One of his slaves, Onesimus, had run away to Rome. During his days in Rome, he met Paul who was in prison at the time. Through Paul's witness, Onesimus became a Christian. Paul sent him back to Philemon bearing an appeal to receive Onesimus, not as a wayward slave, but as a welcomed brother. "Welcome him as you would welcome me," wrote Paul, "for the Lord is the Master of us all." In his ministry Paul worked toward the unity of God's people, challenging the accepted norms whenever possible and breaking down barriers wherever found.

Christ has destroyed the barriers that separate us.
Why is it we keep trying to rebuild them?

Broken Barriers

Philemon
Based on Paul's concerns for Onesimus

Today as I looked about our company
  I was filled with both amazement and joy.
Gathered together in fellowship
  and praise was a most unlikely group...
        singing in unison,
        sitting side by side,
        sharing in a common meal were both
        the educated and the illiterate
        the influential and the unimportant
        the powerful and the oppressed
        the circumcised and the uncircumcised
        the strong and the weak
        the wealthy and the poor
        the free and the slave...

I marvel at the power of the Gospel to bring such a disparate
band together in a spirit of oneness.

Here, there are no division, no barriers,
for Christ is all, and is in all.   Colossians 3:11

Prejudice is banished
Prestige is unimportant
Place and status are put aside.
What prevails is God's Spirit of unity.

              Christ makes us one!
          One in body and one in spirit,
          just as we were called to one hope,
          one Lord, one faith, one baptism,
            one God and Father of all,
      who is over all and through all and in all.
                Ephesians 4:4-5

Amazement and joy fill my heart
    at the sight of such a fellowship!

When Onesimus stood to lead us in prayer,
I was persuaded by the moving of the Spirit to write to
his master, my dear friend and fellow worker, Philemon.
Onesimus came to us as one who was a runaway slave—
        without status,
        without hope,
        without Christ.

Now he is a child of God,
        full of hope,
        and united in Christ
Yet, he remains a slave.
        Unfortunately, still a slave of a man—
            (this is to my sadness);
        Fortunately, a slave of Jesus Christ—
            (this is to my great joy).

There is but one true Master who is in heaven,
        and there is no favoritism with him. Ephesians 6:9

I will send Onesimus back to Philemon as a slave
        (legally that is his status),
        but also as my dear brother
            and as a brother in the Lord.

Because of his faith in the Lord Jesus
and his love for all the saints,
Philemon will refresh my heart
and receive Onesimus as if he were me.

I am confident of this
        because I am confident of the sanctifying power
        of the grace of my Lord Jesus Christ.

Prayer

God and Father of all,
  who is over all and through all and in all—
it was the prayer of Your Son
that all who believe in Him might be one,
just as You and Your Son are one.   John 17:21

May we,
  as Your redeemed people,
  be brought to complete unity.   John 17:23
May we,
  as Your renewed people, be like-minded, having the same
  love, being one in spirit and purpose.   Philippians. 2:2
May we,
  as your ransomed people, make every effort to keep the
  unity of the Spirit through the bond of peace.   Ephesians 4:3
May all the barriers that divide us be removed through Your
  Spirit of reconciliation.

Build up the body of Christ until we all reach
  unity in the faith and in the knowledge of Your Son.

Make us mature,
  attaining to the whole measure of the fullness of Christ.
                                            Ephesians 4:13

Teach us to bear with each other
  and forgive whatever grievance
  we may have against one another.
Teach us to forgive as the Lord forgave us.
Teach us to put on love,
  which binds us together in perfect unity.

      And may the peace of Christ rule in our hearts.
                Colossians 3:13-15

                Amen.

Entry 28

Concerning the death of Paul, our sources are not conclusive. Tradition affirms that Paul was released after a two-year imprisonment. Perhaps he returned to the provinces of the Eastern Mediterranean, or set sail to Spain. We are uncertain. Some scholars suggested that Paul may have been exiled. Whether released or exiled, he was arrested and imprisoned a second time in Rome, this time in more stringent quarters.

On the night of July 18 in A. D. 64, a fire broke out in Rome. The fire lasted five days, destroying much of the city. Many suspected that Nero ordered the fire so he might redesign the city. Faced with such accusations, he looked for a scapegoat. His eye fell upon the Christians. At this point, the persecution of the Christians increased in the imperial city. It was probably during this time that Paul was prosecuted and found guilty, it may be, of being a leader of the Christians and a disturber of the peace.

For Paul, his death meant his release:
"For to me to die is gain...
I desire to depart and be with Christ, which is better by far...
I have fought the good fight, I have finished the race,
I have kept the faith.
Now there is in store for me the crown of righteousness..."
Philippians 1:21 and II Timothy 4; 8-8

There is great joy in finishing
the race and hearing the words of Christ,
"Well done, good and faithful servant!
Come and share your master's happiness."
Matthew 25:21

Confident of This!

II Timothy 4:16-18
Based on Paul's correspondence from prison in Rome.

My dungeon is dank and dreary.
The dampness of the night air blowing in from the coast,
chills my body
and sends an ache
into my bones.

The cold chains around my wrists
and ankles cause my hands to tremble
and my feet to swell.   II Timothy 2:9

Like a common criminal,
I've been discarded by all—

Deserted—
even by my brothers in the faith!   II Timothy 1:15; 4:16

My life has reached the point where soon
it will be sacrificed;
The time of my departure is at hand.

Soon the chains of this mortal body
shall be unfettered;
This earthly body shall see decay and perish;
This body sown in weakness shall be no more.
                    I Corinthians 15:42-43

Yet at my end,
the Lord is still at my side.

It is He that gives me strength;
It is He that rescues me
from the lion's mouth.
It is He that will bring me safely
to his heavenly kingdom.   II Timothy 4:18

Throughout my journey
from the day I met Jesus on the road to Damascus—
to this day as a prisoner in Rome,
I am confident of this!

As I die with him, I will also live with him!
If I endure the hardships of this life I will also reign with him!
II Timothy 2:11

Prayer

Merciful and gracious God,
Long ago, You called me as Your servant;
From that day,
when I heard Your voice call out my name,
I have placed my life
into Your hands to do Your holy will.
I have never been disappointed!

Even now,
as I face this dark hour,
I am confident that You are able to guard
what I have entrusted to You for that future glorious
day of the appearing of my Savior,
Christ Jesus,
who has destroyed death and has brought life
and immortality to light through the gospel.
II Timothy 1:12

You began a good work in me, Your humble servant.
And I have no doubt that what You have begun,
You will carry through unto completion—
until the day of Christ Jesus
to the glory and honor
and praise of God.
Philippians 1:6

Amen!

139

Entry 29

How did Paul die? Tradition states that Paul was beheaded at Aquae Salviae, today called Tre Fontane. This was located at the third milestone on the Ostian Way.

Where was Paul buried? The earliest recorded witness to his burial place comes at the end of second century in a letter written by Gaius, an elder of Rome. He mentions in a correspondence to Proclus of Phrygia that he can point out the memorial monuments of the Apostles Peter and Paul, both claimed by the Roman church as its joint founders. He states that Peter's monument was situated on the Vatican Hill and Paul's was located on the Ostian Way.

On this same site in 324, Constantine constructed a small basilica in commemoration of Paul's apostleship and martyrdom. Near the end of the fourth century, a larger basilica was built that was ravaged by fire in 1823. In 1854, Pope Pius IX reconsecrated the church that continues to stand as a testimony to the mission, ministry, and martyrdom of Paul.

Yet, the greatest monument to Paul's life is not that of stone and mortar but the witnessing Church—

> *"built on the foundation of the apostles and prophets,*
> *with Christ Jesus as the chief cornerstone.*
> *In Him the whole building is joined together*
> *and rises to become a holy temple in the Lord."*
> Ephesians 2:20, 21

May it be said of us that we, too,
built upon Christ through our work produced by faith,
our labor prompted by love,
and our endurance inspired by hope in the Lord.
I Thessalonians 1:3

Our Prayer

Colossians 3:1-17
Based on Paul's Guidelines for Holy Living

Prayer

Gracious God, we thank you for the Apostle Paul.
We thank you for his faithfulness and endurance.
Help us to be faithful and to run the race with renewed strength.

We thank you for his willingness to pour out his heart
and his life for the sake of others.
Help us to possess the heart of a servant, clothed in compassion,
kindness, humility, gentleness and patience.

We thank you for his words of wisdom and instruction.
May we set our hearts on things above and be corrected by
God's words of discipline.

We thank you that he broke down barriers of race,
gender, and class.
May we, too, reach out across all fences that separate us from
one another.

We thank you that Paul proclaimed the gospel of grace
through faith in Jesus Christ.
Help us to live grace-filled lives, bearing with one another,
forgiving one another as the Lord forgave us. And over all,
may we put on love.

May all that we do, whether in word or deed, be done in such a
way that the name of the Lord Jesus will be praised,
and thanksgiving be given to You through Him.

This we ask through Jesus Christ, our Savior and Lord.
Amen.

Order Information

Give the Gift of
The Journal of Paul

It's the perfect gift for friends and family who want to deepen their experience and insights into one of the greatest missionaries of the church, the Apostle Paul.

For only $12.95 (plus shipping and handling) you'll receive this informative and inspiring devotional book. Call today: phone/fax 1-972-418-6103, email-GrkCen@aol.com

Or write:
The Greek Center for Biblical Studies
2308 York Ct.
Carrollton, Texas 75006

Volume discounts available for multiple quantities.

The Greek Center for Biblical Studies specializes in travel tours to Greece, Turkey, Italy and Israel following the journeys of the Apostle Paul. Dr. Sparks, along with his wife, Elizabeth, lead several tours annually. For more information concerning these tours or to book Dr. Sparks as a guest speaker, contact the Greek Center for Biblical Studies.